Goldkeeper

Sally Prue

OXFORD
UNIVERSITY PRESS

Chapter 1

Its eyes saw everything.

It saw every tiptoeing verger, and every humble worshipper, and every baby being offered to its god. Everyone was swept by the tiger-stone gaze of the great statue.

And over them all, as delicate as an eggshell, the vast dome of the Temple hung.

The family in the doorway faltered, but there was no turning back.

They made their way gently across the honey-coloured tiles, and the baby's new eyes gazed, fascinated, at the gilded vanes that spun beneath the delicate lamps.

The family stopped under the eyes of the great statue. The High Priest (for it was he, himself, and not the apprentice) took a step forwards to the Bowl of Offering, and the million fragments of gold that covered his robe flashed dazzlingly before their eyes.

He asked a gruff question, and reached out a hand towards the child.

But the child let out a cry, a shrill scream that pierced the sun-shafted gloom of the Temple and bounced off every gilded leaf and chiselled bee until the air was thick with buzzing echoes. And the gold coin the baby had been clutching spun up and up, flashing and vanishing and flashing again, until it fell with a harsh *clang!* and was lost to sight.

One of the vergers let out a cry.

'An omen!' she cried. 'The baby has refused to make its Offering! It must be cursed!'

But the baby's sister, a bright girl of some six years of age, said, 'Look!' And they all looked; and there, in the great hand of the statue of the god Ora, was lodged the gold coin.

And there was much wonder amongst them all. The parents of the child felt even more certain the baby must be of particular intelligence and importance, though its brothers and sister were almost certain the whole thing was an accident and *so not fair*.

The baby's great-aunts were extremely offended by the whole affair. They stomped dourly back to the party that was being held in the baby's honour, sniffed grudgingly at the sandwiches and muttered dark things about the baby causing trouble to everyone.

But its mother was a modern, enlightened parent who already had three beautifully behaved, intelligent children. She put the baby into a frilly basket with a tape of a walrus' stomach-rumblings to listen to. She'd done the same with the others, and they'd all turned out beautifully.

'He'll cause disaster and mayhem!' sniffed one of the great-aunts, on her way to the bathroom. 'I can feel it in my bones!'

But the baby's father, who was an architect, had just got an even better job and so it was plain that this was a lucky child.

And the City was so golden and peaceful in those days that you could almost *feel* the great god Ora's tiger-stone eyes shining on you as you went about the City.

Mr and Mrs Blewitt settled back to watch baby Sebastian blossom.

Things didn't turn out quite as planned.

Chapter 2

'Ooh!' said Ellie. 'Look!'

A golden limousine was turning into the school drive.

'I know who that is,' said Dora Payne, importantly. 'That's the High Priest of Ora, that is, looking for a new apprentice for the Temple.'

Sebastian eyed the limousine with sudden hope. Perhaps the High Priest would choose his brother Edward. Edward was Head of Year, and, except for the fact that the High Priest's apprentice was usually an orphan, Edward was just the type for a responsible job like that.

'Back to your work, everyone!' boomed Mr Walty. 'The High Priest isn't going to be very impressed if he sees you all gawping out of the window.'

They all looked at each other.

'Will he come in here, sir?' asked Rory, suddenly uncertain.

'Unless he finds the apprentice in another class first, yes, I expect he will.'

There was a pause while everybody took this in.

'Will he have his stick-things with him, sir?'

'His golden divining rods. Yes, that's right.'

'Ora loves gold, doesn't He,' said Ellie. 'That's why we take gold to the Temple for Him.'

'How do the divining rods work?' asked Jordan.

'Well, when they are pointed at the person who's going to be the next apprentice, Ora will make the little spheres at the ends glow red.'

'I bet he chooses me,' said Horace, smugly.

Horace could get away with saying things like that, partly because he was an orphan, and partly because his uncle was Mr Meeno and people who weren't nice to Mr Meeno tended to be terribly unlucky about stepping into big blocks of concrete and then falling in the river.

'But, sir,' said Rory, 'if Ora chooses the next apprentice Himself, then it doesn't matter whether we're working or not, does it?'

Mr Walty smiled very slightly.

'Possibly not to Ora, bless His holy name,' he said. 'But the headmaster will not be at all pleased if you make a bad impression on the High Priest and I myself will be incandescent with rage if you make a bad impression on the headmaster. So if I were you, I'd get back to work.'

People considered, sighed, and sat back down. No one got on the wrong side of Mr Walty if they could help it. Their parents kept telling them that he was ever such a nice man, but they knew better.

Teachers were like that. Treacherous.

Sebastian drew a circle on his piece of paper. They were supposed to be drawing autumn fruits, but by the time Sebastian had finished sharpening his pencil really properly, all that'd been left in the box was a hard round thing like an undernourished conker.

Sebastian got out his penknife and began to cut into the fruit.

It was ever so hard. The penknife had skidded off and made several gouges in his table before he could prise the thing open.

It was full of tiny seeds. Sebastian was just wondering whether it would be more satisfying to flick them at Horace, or else drop them down Horace's neck, when he suddenly realized that the seeds were moving. Yes, now he looked carefully he could see that they weren't seeds at all, but tiny black beetles. They must have holed themselves up in the fruit ready for the winter.

It was rather flattering to be master of a hundred or so beetles. Sebastian picked up the pieces of his fruit and wandered over to the girls' table.

'Look,' said Sebastian.

Dora Payne looked.

'What is it?'

'My fruit. I cut it open. See?'

Dora's eyes widened. 'Mr Walty will give you a detention,' she said, very pleased. 'Look what he's done,

Horace! He's spoiled his fruit.'

Horace looked smug and vicious at the same time.

'Mr Walty will send you to the headmaster,' he said, with relish. 'And *then* you'll be in trouble!'

Sebastian took no notice. People were always saying things like that. You just had to ignore them.

'Here,' he said, and tipped the contents of one half of the fruit carefully onto Dora's hand.

'Mr Walty!' she said. 'Mr Walty!'

But Mr Walty was arranging a display on the other side of the classroom and took no notice.

Dora must have frightened the beetles, for they were pretending to be seeds again.

'Mr Walty,' called Horace, nastily. 'Look what Sebastian's done!'

And then some brave beetle decided it'd better find somewhere quieter to hibernate.

Dora looked down as she felt the movement on her hand – and her eyes bulged.

'Ooh!' she said, sharply, as if someone had poked her. 'They're alive! Ooh. They're alive! Ooh!'

All the other girls got up and moved away hastily, saying things like, 'Oh, Sebastian' and 'How could you?' but Dora sat rock still, gazing incredulously at her hand.

'They're crawling about!' she whispered, as if she could hardly believe it. 'They're all crawling about!

Stop it! Stop it!'

Mr Walty came storming across the room.

'What's the meaning of all this?' he demanded. 'Sebastian Blewitt – '

'It's crawling up my arm!' howled Dora. 'AAARGH!'

And then she screamed so loudly you could see right down her throat to the wiggly thing, and she shook her hand.

The beetles went everywhere.

'Watch what you're doing!' said Sebastian, indignantly, as it rained beetles.

All the girls were running in circles, panicking. 'There's one in my hair!' screeched Ellie. 'I felt one! I felt one! One landed in my hair!'

Everyone was standing up now to watch. Mr Walty was doing his nut.

'Sit *down*!' he bellowed. 'Every one of you sit down at *once*. At once, do you hear?'

But people were jumping up and down and searching each other for beetles, and Dora was on her chair with her hands to her head, shrieking, and sort of running on the spot.

Sebastian went down on his hands and knees and started an anxious rescue mission. He picked each beetle up very carefully on Dora's drawing and slid it into Ellie's pencil tin.

Mr Walty was actually dancing with rage.

'Everyone be quiet!' he bellowed.

And, suddenly, everyone was.

'Dora, how dare you make such a noise!'

Dora's eyes went round with incredulous, wounded, innocence.

'But Sebastian – '

'And get down from that chair at once!'

'Sebastian put black beetles all over her,' pointed out Horace, smugly, as, highly tragic and affronted, Dora got down.

'Poor Dora,' said Ellie.

'Yes,' said Jordan. 'Look, I found one in Ellie's hair.'

'And I'm sure I got one down my neck!' piped up Rory, pathetically.

'And there're loads more all over Sebastian's table,' said Horace.

There was a swift movement away from it.

Mr Walty stood and breathed for several seconds.

'I see,' he said flatly. 'Sebastian Blewitt!'

Sebastian coaxed another beetle into Ellie's pencil-case, but he could tell he was in trouble by the way Mr Walty's nostril hairs were bristling.

Mr Walty began to speak in dangerously quiet bursts, like a kettle coming to the boil.

'What – do you think – you were doing – throwing beetles – all over the classroom?'

'I didn't,' said Sebastian.

All the girls began squealing.

'Oh, but he did!'

'It was all his fault!'

'I feel shuddery all over.'

'BE QUIET!' Mr Walty waited until the echoes had died away from the rafters before he began again.

'You horrible little boy! How dare you disrupt my class by bringing those disgusting creatures in here!'

'I didn't,' said Sebastian.

'Be quiet!'

The beetles were trying to climb out of the pencil tin, but luckily the sides were too shiny. Their little legs were going like mad, and Sebastian suddenly felt really sorry for them. He'd have to do up the fruit with sticky tape as soon as he could and put it back outside.

Mr Walty was getting personal.

'I have taught your sister,' he said. 'I have taught both of your brothers–fine, hard-working, intelligent children who were a credit to their classes. But as for *you*, Sebastian Blewitt – '

Or perhaps string would be better. He didn't want the beetles getting stuck to the tape.

'Are you listening to me, boy?'

Sebastian discovered that Mr Walty had gone ever such a funny colour, a bit like strawberry yogurt.

'Not really,' he said and Mr Walty's face deepened instantly to the richest black cherry.

'You horrible boy!' he bellowed. 'I've had enough of you, do you hear? You are insolent, you are inattentive, you are incorrigibly lazy. Well, I've had enough of you disrupting the class. From now on – '

'Mr Walty!'

It wasn't spoken loudly, but something about the tone got through. Mr Walty froze in mid-bellow and went all mottled, like a cuttlefish. Then he swivelled round and gaped, and everyone else swivelled round and gaped, too.

The headmaster was always an awe-inspiring sight in his blood-red gown and gold-tasselled mortar board, but at that moment no one had eyes for him, because standing with him in the doorway was a man in robes that were shining with thousands of sequins of gold.

Chapter 3

Everyone gasped in wonder and embarrassment, and a sort of whisper passed over the room: *the High Priest*.

'Oh,' said Mr Walty, in a strangled voice. 'I didn't hear you. Um. I beg your pardon.'

The headmaster ground his teeth. The room was so quiet that everyone heard it.

'His Omniscience the High Priest of Ora has come to inspect the pupils of the school,' he growled.

Mr Walty started babbling.

'Ah. Yes. Yes, of course. An honour. A great honour. We were just ... er ... doing some artwork on our fruits project. Please do come in and ... er ... help yourself, Your Omniscience. Er ... mind the beetles.'

Sebastian had hardly ever seen the High Priest, because usually when you got dragged along to the Temple you only got to see the apprentice. And the High Priest was worth seeing. He had watery eyes that blinked nervously above a vivid blob of a nose, and he was holding two gold sticks jutting out in front of him.

Everybody gawped like goldfish: it was the High Priest, who helped Ora and the Council rule the City and who knew the secrets of the gold vaults.

'This is Middle Seven,' the headmaster was saying, grimly. 'Yes ... er ... do mind the beetles, Your Omniscience.'

The High Priest heaved himself massively to the front of the classroom. Then he turned, and waved his divining rods in front of the class. The gold sticks flashed as they caught a sudden beam of sunshine.

Horace had a big fat smirk all over his greasy face.

'Of course, these are some of our younger children,' the headmaster was saying. 'Perhaps if you were to visit one of our older classes – '

The golden sticks bobbed violently, and everybody jumped. The High Priest blinked his rheumy eyes.

'Something,' he said. 'I believe I just registered something, Headmaster.'

The High Priest began to sweep his rods from side to side. No one breathed. Everyone was so petrified that Sebastian took the opportunity to get down on the floor to round up the rest of the beetles.

The rods leapt again, bucking in the High Priest's flabby hands.

'Does this mean you may have found someone suitable?' asked the headmaster, failing to hide his incredulity.

'The force is very strong,' said the High Priest. 'Certainly very strong indeed. There's no one here wearing an old luminous watch, is there?'

They all looked round at each other, vastly impressed. Horace began edging his way to the front. His grin was so broad that the top of his head was in danger of falling off.

'I believe not,' said the headmaster, having swept the room with professionally suspicious eyes.

'Ah,' said the High Priest. 'He's somewhere close, then. Somewhere very close.'

'Your Omniscience's apprentice?' said the headmaster, quite staggered.

'In this room. Yes.'

Two people began to cry, and several more puffed out their chests and looked pleased with themselves. The most pleased of them all was Horace. He stood with his hands on his hips and his little button eyes shining as bright as beetles.

Sebastian reckoned that if the High Priest kept on dithering about then he'd be able to slip out and put the beetles in the hedge without anyone noticing. He'd only got to check the legs of Dora's table, now.

Everyone else in the class was frozen into tingling silence. The only sound was the flopping of the High Priest's embroidered slippers as he got closer and closer to Horace's grin.

Flop. Flop-flop. Flop-flop.

'I think it's me, sir!'

'Be quiet, Jordan.'

Flop.

'Very close, now,' said the High Priest, shifting his great bulk uneasily. 'The power's amazing.'

He shuffled to a halt. The golden divining rods were pointing straight at Horace's chest, and the air nearly cracked with tension.

'I believe – ' began the High Priest.

That was every last beetle. Sebastian, relieved, got quietly to his feet – and the sacred divining rods jumped in the High Priest's big hands.

He clutched at them, even for a moment seemed to be trying to pull them back, but the rods slipped through his hands until they were pointing straight at Sebastian's belly-button.

And suddenly the spheres on the ends were glowing bright, bright red.

Horace let out a squawk.

'Not *him*!' he said.

'Great Ora!' breathed the High Priest, staring at the divining rods in amazement.

Sebastian suddenly found himself the centre of attention.

'What?' he said.

'The sacred divining rods!' whispered the High Priest.

'What about them?'

'*Sebastian Blewitt!*' hissed Mr Walty.

'What?'

'It's ... it's incredible,' muttered the High Priest, shifting his wobbly bulk from one foot to another. 'The rods wouldn't have it. There was nothing I could do. *Nothing* I could do! Oh, great Ora, great Ora, great Ora preserve me!'

Horace snarled, and stepped forward between the divining rods and Sebastian. At once the red lights at the end of the rods blinked out.

'No,' said the High Priest, shaking his head. 'It's not you. I tried my best, but it's not. It's *him*. That boy with the beetles. It's him. *He's* the new apprentice.'

Mr Walty and the headmaster exchanged appalled glances.

'Perhaps we ought to search Blewitt's pockets,' murmured Mr Walty. 'You know: for luminous watches.'

'This isn't one of our most trustworthy boys,' said the headmaster, very worried. 'I'd hate for there to be any mistake.'

The High Priest drew out a limp square of gold satin and patted his forehead.

'No. No, there can't be,' he said. His face was moist and white and bewildered. 'It's the power of Ora, bless His holy name. I've never felt anything like it. It's exploding from him like ... like exploding things.'

And the headmaster looked at the High Priest searchingly, sighed, and gave up.

'Very well,' he said. 'Of course you know your business best, Your Omniscience. If you're quite sure ...'

'I'll tell my uncle!' said Horace, loudly and accusingly.

The High Priest jumped, and blinked round at Horace's greasy, accusing scowl.

'But it's the power,' he said again, almost beseechingly. 'Ora, bless His holy name, has chosen him. That's it, you see: there's nothing any of us can do. No one could fight it, not if he was Councillor Kimber himself.'

The High Priest mopped his brow again.

'Perhaps you'd arrange for his belongings to be gathered together, Headmaster. And then I can take him with me.'

Chapter 4

'Here,' said Sebastian, indignantly, looking round at all the shocked faces around him. 'What's he going on about?'

Mr Walty's face assumed a ghastly smile.

'You've been chosen, boy,' he explained.

'What?'

'As High Priest's apprentice, boy. So, get your things together, and His Omniscience will take you to the Temple.'

'What?' said Sebastian, hotly. 'Just a flaming minute! You must be joking!'

Mr Walty began taking things out of Sebastian's locker.

'It's a great, a huge honour,' he said. 'We'll miss you, of course – ' here he failed to suppress a huge seraphic smile, ' – but we'll have to try to bear our loss cheerfully.'

Sebastian scowled, and put his hands on his hips.

'Now look here,' he said, 'I'm not going to be anybody's apprentice! I'm going to be a gangster, I am, when I grow up. I've got it all planned.'

Mr Walty was still taking things out of Sebastian's locker.

'A gangster,' Sebastian went on, doggedly. 'We're going to have our own hideout and be gangsters, Gerald and me.'

'Fancy *him* being High Priest's apprentice,' said Dora, in disgust.

'Those divining rods must have gone wrong,' said Horace, dangerously.

'Would you like to take your tree-sculpture with you?' asked Mr Walty.

'No,' said Sebastian.

'Well, then. Say goodbye to Sebastian, Class Seven, and wish him luck in his new life.'

'Goodbye, Sebastian,' said everyone drearily. 'Good luck, Sebastian.' But there was a hiss amongst the sing-song, and it said, '*My uncle's going to kill you.*'

'Come along, then, Blewitt!'

Sebastian didn't budge. He stood and scowled.

'Now look here,' he said, 'if I go with the High Priest, does that mean I don't have to come to school any more?'

Mr Walty's face split into a smile of rapture.

'That's right, my boy. No school.'

'And I get to ride in the limo?'

'Yes, yes.'

Sebastian nodded.

'OK,' he said. 'I'll give it a go, then.'

And he picked up Ellie's tin of beetles and made his way out of the classroom without a backward glance.

The limo was brilliant: Bert, the driver, wore a peaked cap, and everybody waved and smiled as they went along, and there was even a drinks cabinet with various revolting paint-strippery liquids and some lemonade in it.

The limo rocked massively round the tight cobbled corners of the City and hummed its way through the elegant garden squares. Quite soon it swerved past a man bearing a placard that read 'BREAK THE CHAINS OF ORA' by the huge pillars of the portico that guarded the entrance to the Temple.

'Cor!' said Sebastian, looking with new interest at the carved bees that swarmed busily over the golden stone, and at the great stone turkey that peered indignantly at everyone who went past.

The limo lumbered round one last corner and slid to a halt. The High Priest was heaving himself out of the car almost before the handbrake had creaked on and by the time Sebastian had found the electric door-opening button the High Priest was burrowing busily in the boot.

There was a heavy suitcase and various plastic bags on the cobbles behind him.

'You going on holiday?' asked Sebastian.

The High Priest's answer was muffled by his huge burrowing backside.

'On retreat. To get away from ... from all the pressure. It's a nice place. Quite pleasant since they've drained the cellars. Not so whiffy. And not even Ora could expect me ... He will be merciful. I'm sure He will be merciful.'

He looked furtively left and right and then heaved his suitcase over to the grubby taxi that was lurking on the other side of the alley.

'Turville will look after you,' he said, throwing the case onto the back seat. He waddled back to the limo, his face mauve with sweat and haste, to seize the plastic bags. 'Er ... tell him I've gone.'

The High Priest threw the bags into the back of the taxi, wrapped his glittering robe closely about his knees, and wedged himself into the front seat.

'Good luck,' he said gruffly. 'Go on round and in the main entrance. Watch out for ... er ... well, good luck, anyway. I'm sure they wouldn't do anything much to a child. Oh, and you'll need these.'

He fished fussily in a carrier bag and handed over a golden box a bit like Sebastian's brother Robert's clarinet case. Then the High Priest slammed the door and the taxi drew away with a roar of holed exhaust and a cloud of choking smoke.

Sebastian shrugged, and made his way back round the Temple wall into the dazzling sunshine of the portico.

The man with the placard stopped when he saw him.

'Oi,' he said. 'What are you doing round here? You should be at school, shouldn't you?'

'Not me,' said Sebastian. 'Not any more. I'm the new apprentice.'

'Come off it, you're too young. Now run off home before you get into trouble.'

'No, I am,' said Sebastian. 'It's brilliant. It means I won't have to go to school any more. Not ever!'

The man looked at him again, more closely: then he shook his head, leant his placard against a golden column, and put his hands on Sebastian's shoulders.

'You needn't do it,' he said, earnestly. 'Look, just walk away, now. You don't want to get mixed up with all that lot. They'll take you to pieces, they will. Brainwash you. Have you living in fear and trembling, a slave to superstition and corruption.'

Sebastian considered.

'Yeah,' he said. 'But I won't have to go to school any more. And, in any case, I've got to hand in the stick-things.'

The man with the placard sighed gently and mournfully and all his wrinkles seemed to settle and deepen. He patted Sebastian on the shoulder.

'Poor lad,' he said. 'Poor lad. Enmeshed in their snares already. But look, young man – '

'Sebastian,' said Sebastian. 'Sebastian Blewitt.'

' – Master Blewitt. You know me, don't you? Finley Wortle. I'm here every day, protesting. A lone voice of reason in a world of fear. So if you ever need help – '

'Yeah, ta,' said Sebastian. 'Thanks a lot, all right?'

He pushed hard at the great door of the Temple and it gave way slowly, heavily, with a wheeze of sealed air.

He slid through the opening and the door closed behind him. All the outside noises: cars, and the flutter of footsteps, and the tumbling jackdaws, sighed into cushiony quietness, and Sebastian was enveloped by a scent of beeswax, cloves, and mildew.

And then the eyes saw him. He felt them, like a brush of fur across his face.

He looked up, and there was the great golden statue: the fine muscles of the chest, the rigid waving of the hair, but most of all the eyes, staring. Ora: ruler and god and worker of miracles.

Sebastian gave him the thumbs-up.

'Wotcha,' he said.

Chapter 5

'What are *you* doing here?' said someone, sharply. An aged face was poking at him out of the shadows. 'Where are your parents?'

Sebastian shrugged. Mrs Blewitt lectured on Whole Health and Women's Issues and Mr Blewitt was an architect, but he tried to keep it quiet.

'At work,' he said.

The woman sniffed. She wore a badge which said MRS L. POASH: VERGER.

'Well, you shouldn't be here unaccompanied,' she said, and began shooing him backwards towards the door. 'Off you go, off you go.'

'Here, hang about!' protested Sebastian. 'I'm *supposed* to be here. I'm the new apprentice, I am. Look, I've got the gold sticks and everything.'

She was so taken aback that even her stiff swirl of hair juddered a bit.

'Great heavens,' she said. 'So soon, and so young!'

'Well, I'm getting older all the time,' pointed out Sebastian, but she only frowned, clacked purposefully past him, and picked up a golden hammer from a niche by the door.

Sebastian hastily put a bit of distance between himself

and the mad old bat.

'Here, watch out,' he said. 'Cor, Finley Wortle was right about you lot, he – '

She raised the hammer to shoulder height, and Sebastian stopped arguing and dived under a table. He was crawling out the other side when the hammer fell: suddenly the whole Temple was filled with an intense *boing-boing-boing*, and the golden gong that hung in the shadows was trembling and casting a flickering spider's web of golden rays all round the great space. Everything was shivering: every fluted railing and elegant lamp and well-filled stomach was vibrating in sympathy. The sound swung round the gloom of the Temple and quivered the glass in every window.

And as the gong faded into nothingness Mrs Poash called out, loud and strong: 'Here is the servant of Ora!'

And all the people answered with one voice: 'Great is the bounty of Ora. Bless His holy name!'

And suddenly Sebastian, peeking over the top of the table, found himself gazing at a hundred bald spots, and a hundred heads of spray-stiffened curls, as everybody in the Temple bowed.

'Councillor Kimber,' murmured someone who looked like a walrus. Most of the people in the Temple looked like walruses, though there were one or two, like

Mrs Poash, who were more like flamingos. They were all very old. Councillor Kimber, on the other hand, was only just middle-aged. He arrived in a brisk whisk of camel coat and shaved shiny cheeks; knife-glanced, bald except for a halo of baby-fuzz, and extremely fit.

'Hi!' said Sebastian, cheerily.

But Councillor Kimber didn't look as though smiling was on his day's agenda.

'Did he bring back the divining rods?' he demanded, sharply.

A walrus bumbled forward and presented the box. 'He's returned them, quite correctly, Councillor.'

'Very well,' said Councillor Kimber, grudgingly. 'Witnesses?'

Someone fumbled eagerly at a folder.

'Sworn statements from the Headmaster, Class Teacher, Whiteboard Monitor, and High Priest,' he said, as excited as someone so old could be without actually doing himself a mischief.

Councillor Kimber gave Sebastian a stiletto glance and zipped his signature under all the others.

'The office of apprentice carries with it a great deal of responsibility,' he said, 'as the High Priest will no doubt – '

He broke off, frowning, and fired another perishing look round the room. 'Where *is* the High Priest?' he asked. 'I would have thought he'd be here for this occasion, at the very least.'

There was a silence while the walruses looked at each other. So Sebastian said, 'He's off on holiday, isn't he?'

Councillor Kimber threw down his pen, and everybody jumped.

'Gone on *holiday*!' he snapped. 'But he can't do that *now*. What does he think he's playing at?'

The mustard gowns of the vergers rustled, like trees before a squall.

'Perhaps the High Priest feels the need for uninterrupted prayer,' suggested a faintly fluttering flamingo.

'You aren't suggesting that there's a better place for prayer than the Temple?' snapped Councillor Kimber. 'Because if that's the case there seems very little point in keeping the place open. Really!' He went on, 'However is the apprentice supposed to be able to perform his duties when he's had no instruction?' He cast a cold eye over Sebastian. 'And he's particularly *small*, as well.'

'Hey!' said Sebastian. 'I'm not small. I'm one of the biggest in my class, I am!'

'I think he's particularly *young*,' said one of the walruses, apologetically.

'That makes it worse! We can't just leave the boy to fend for himself.'

'You should see Horace Meeno,' went on Sebastian. 'I'm three inches taller than him, I am. More, even. *He's* so weedy he looks as if he's made out of knotted spaghetti.'

'I suppose I can assign him one of the Council bodyguards,' went on Councillor Kimber, unheeding. 'But they're hardly trained to act as nursemaids.'

'Oi!' said Sebastian, but the door at the far end of the room was opening and someone new was coming in.

The young man paused in the doorway, looked round at the crowd of ancient people, put his hands together, and beamed.

'Goodness,' he said, 'fancy finding him already! Haven't you all done just *marvellously* well?'

The walruses perked up, and even the flamingos smirked a little, but Councillor Kimber only scowled.

'It's not well at all, Turville,' he snapped. 'The High Priest's taken himself off somewhere and I'm left with this ... this *infant*!'

'Here, hang about,' said Sebastian, scowling. 'I'm not an infant! I left Infants years ago. I'm not in Juniors, even. You just watch what – '

But the young man walked right up to Sebastian and held out his hand. He wore a neat white apron over a cherry-coloured suit and he had a slim ring on every finger.

'I'm afraid this is all ever such a palaver,' he said, confidingly. 'But we'll soon sort everything out. And don't mind Councillor Kimber, here. He's a lovely man, but just ever so busy and important.'

Councillor Kimber cleared his throat.

'Look, Turville,' he said, 'now I come to think about it, I suppose you're the one to look after the apprentice, here. Get him settled in. Make sure he does his duties, and all that sort of thing.'

Turville flicked back his fair hair and regarded Sebastian with warm hazel eyes.

'Oh yes, Councillor Kimber,' he said. 'Why, of course I will. That'll be just the hugest pleasure of all.'

Chapter 6

Mrs Blewitt placed a plate of baked beans on toast very reverently on the table in front of Sebastian.

'I'll ring out for a pizza or something, usually,' Sebastian explained. 'Or else Turville will cook for me.'

'Have you got your own phone?' asked Eunice, sharply.

'Yeah. Two.'

Tears filled Mrs Blewitt's eyes.

'I'm so proud of you,' she said mistily. 'Two phones!'

'One only gets through to Councillor Kimber, though.'

Edward whistled.

'You've got a hotline to Councillor Kimber?'

'What's he like?' demanded Eunice.

Sebastian considered: he hadn't really taken much notice.

'All right,' he said.

'But he must really hate you. He's totally opposed to the Temple's having power over the City. Especially since the High Priest got that law changed so they can build a casino right next to the Temple.'

'Yeah. Councillor Kimber, he seemed to have the hump, a bit. I've got my own fridge so I can always have ice-cream and stuff.'

Mr Blewitt came in waving a bottle.

'To celebrate!' he said, grinning through his beard.

'Is it lemonade?' asked Sebastian. Mrs Blewitt didn't approve of fizzy drinks, generally, because of their teeth.

'Not exactly.'

'Oh.'

Mrs Blewitt hadn't stopped smiling since Sebastian had arrived home in the limo.

'He's got two phones,' she said. 'And his own fridge.'

'And a huge bedroom,' said Sebastian. 'All to myself. With a television and an entertainment centre with multi-region maxi discs and everything.'

Edward and Robert exchanged glances.

'I don't believe in having a television in your bedroom,' said Robert, stiffly. 'I think it interferes with your social competence.' But he said it without conviction.

'Your bedroom?' echoed Mrs Blewitt, stopping smiling for the first time. 'But … but you won't be *sleeping* at the Temple, darling, will you?'

'Yep,' said Sebastian, shovelling down baked beans. 'Except Tuesdays and Saturdays. I have to come home then.'

'Why?' asked Edward.

'Dunno. Nights off, I suppose. Didn't ask.'

'Oh, but – ' began Mrs Blewitt. 'Oh, but – oh, Sebastian.'

Mr Blewitt patted her hand.

'We must be very brave, dear,' he said, quietly. 'It's the will of Ora, after all. Herbal herb drink, Sebastian? It's organic.'

'No,' said Sebastian. 'I'm going to have a chat to Gerald. He's never been in a limo before. It's got electric doors and a footbath with bubbles.'

'You won't be able to take Gerald,' said Eunice, with swift satisfaction. 'He won't be allowed in the Temple. Will he, Mummy?'

'Oh dear,' said Mrs Blewitt. 'I'm afraid not, darling. Not even to visit. Still, I expect Robert and Edward would look after Gerald for you, Sebastian.'

'Oh no they wouldn't,' said Sebastian. 'Not properly. They wouldn't talk to him, would they?'

Robert laughed hollowly.

'To Gerald? What about? Pest control?'

'Oh dear,' said Mrs Blewitt, again. 'Perhaps – '

The door closed on her words. Sebastian had gone out to find some more intelligent company. Gerald was waiting for him.

'Brought you a biscuit from the Temple,' said Sebastian, gruffly. 'Got icing on it, and everything.'

Sweet things were rare in the Blewitt household: Robert was going to be a doctor, and Mrs Blewitt lectured on Whole Health, and so they all lived on rabbit food. Even Gerald.

'But it isn't natural,' Sebastian had protested. 'I mean, I've never seen any of this seed stuff growing in the whole

City. So it can't be, can it? Huh?'

Robert had looked lordly. His ability to do this was one of the most irritating things about him.

'The thing is, Sebastian – '

'What we should really do,' said Sebastian, 'to be really natural, is to let Gerald scavenge wherever he wants.'

Edward blinked through his glasses. He was going to be a professor, and knew everything. 'He'd leave droppings all over the kitchen. Mum'd freak.'

But the idea of Gerald free to explore the house was an enchanting one.

'I could house-train him,' said Sebastian.

'He'd eat through the telephone wire again. Or he'd get into the bin and get thrown out with the rubbish.'

That was an appalling thought.

'I could train him to come, then,' said Sebastian, doggedly. 'So we could make sure where he was before we threw anything out.'

'Sort of homing rat,' said Edward, and sniggered.

'Yeah,' said Sebastian, eagerly. 'I bet he'd be a brilliant homer. We could get loads of people and do races just like they do with pigeons.'

He stopped to imagine it: hundreds of ordinary fat white rats waddling along earnestly; and then, like a streak of lightning, Gerald, the wild, the sleek, the indomitable.

Sebastian paused to wonder if Mr Blewitt would let him have a cabinet for all Gerald's trophies.

‘I could give him training runs round the house,’ he said.

‘You’d better be jolly careful what Gerald does,’ said Robert, ‘or Mum won’t let you keep him.’

And Sebastian, sighing, had had to admit that was sound advice.

Sebastian never understood his family’s attitude to Gerald. They collected money for Guide Dogs and Cruelty To Animals, but when they were presented with a real live animal – an orphan, too – they hadn’t been at all welcoming. In fact, Sebastian suspected it was only because Mr and Mrs Blewitt had been so worried about gangsters shutting down Mr Blewitt’s job that he’d managed to persuade them to let Gerald stay.

Gerald had been rescued from the terrier at No. 26. Sebastian had arrived almost too late – the whole yard filled with the most horrible slaughter – but he’d found one youngster who’d managed to crawl away from its wrecked nest to hide behind a flowerpot. And that had been Gerald. Gerald, Sebastian’s best friend. The most intelligent rat in the world.

Sebastian found a suitcase on top of Mr Blewitt’s wardrobe. He made several holes in the leather with his penknife, for air, put in a bit of hay and rat mix, and Gerald went into it quite happily. Then Sebastian was ready to go, except for Mrs Blewitt's fussing about toothbrushes and his Ambitions Book. All the Blewitts had their own Ambitions Book. Mrs Blewitt herself wrote *Became High Priest's apprentice* under his own last entry, which was *Find out what frogspawn tastes like*.

'Right,' said Sebastian. 'I'll be off, then.'

Mrs Blewitt wound Sebastian's scarf tenderly round his neck.

'Goodbye, darling,' she whispered. 'I'll come and see you tomorrow.'

'No, not tomorrow. They're showing me the ropes tomorrow ... I think you must sort of swing from them.'

Mr Blewitt put a hand on his wife's shoulder and said something serious about letting the boy find his feet.

'Until Saturday, then,' said Mrs Blewitt, sorrowfully.

'That's only two days,' pointed out Eunice, who was going to be a barrister and was probably even cleverer than Robert and Edward.

Sebastian sank back into the luxurious leather of the limo.

'Yeah,' he said. 'See you around, all right?'

They'd just turned the corner when the car's engine exploded.

It would have been quite nasty if they hadn't been crossing the canal: the burning engine burst up through the bonnet, did a somersault, and crashed down sizzlingly into the water. Fortunately, the accompanying splash put out the flames under the car just before they reached the petrol tank.

Bert sat and stared straight ahead for quite some time. When the smoke cleared it turned out he'd gone the colour of lard.

Sebastian had to ride back to the Temple in a police car, so that was nice.

And, best of all, he got to wave at Horace, who just happened to be hanging about by the side of the road.

Chapter 7

Sebastian woke in his huge bed to the sound of scrabbling and steady, determined gnawing. He pulled Mr Blewitt's suitcase out from under his bed and found that a pair of strong yellow teeth were busily enlarging one of the air holes.

Turville came tripping in bearing a heap of clothes, and Sebastian hurriedly slid the case back under the bed.

'Sacred robes, Your Knowingness,' Turville trilled. 'All nice and fresh. We're lucky we had a set small enough, really.'

The robe was red, with gold frilly bits, and it looked like a toy soldier's nightie. They must be joking. Sebastian looked around.

'Oi, where are my jeans?' he demanded. 'I threw them down safely in that corner last night, and now someone's gone and pinched them!'

'Oh dear,' said Turville. 'Didn't anyone tell you? I've burned them.'

'What?'

'Well, it's traditional,' said Turville. 'I'm afraid the robes are all you've got now, my love.'

Sebastian scowled. He'd look like a wassail tree if he put those robes on. Worse than that, he'd look like a wassail tree that had been decorated by a *girl*. There was no way he was walking around like that and in any case, he hadn't found anywhere to hide Gerald.

'I resign,' he said. 'Call the limo.'

All Turville's bangles jangled as he clutched at his fine fair hair in horror.

'Oh, but you can't!' he exclaimed. 'Why, you've been chosen. Chosen by the sacred divining rods, by Ora himself. You're the one who's been chosen to be the High Priest's apprentice. Oh, and we do need you; we're in such trouble!'

'Are you? What sort of trouble?'

Turville rolled his eyes.

'Gangsters,' he said, dramatically.

Sebastian felt a flicker of interest.

'What, Mr Meeno and all that?'

Turville shuddered. 'A whole group of them,' he said. 'People are saying they're planning to take over the whole City. Ooh, and we don't know what they'll do next … And then there's all this casino business, as well. That's got the whole Council in such a fervour, bless them.'

'A casino? What, dice and cards and stuff?'

Turville nodded.

'Right on the sacred hill. It might even upset the plans for the new shopping mall, and oh, that would be such a pity.'

Sebastian considered. Having a casino over the road

sounded quite fun; and having Mr Meeno and a few gangsters around might add a bit of character and excitement to the place. There was room for everyone, he reckoned–except possibly Horace.

'Councillor Kimber did look a bit of a misery-guts,' he observed. 'Probably not much of a one for games and stuff.'

'Oh, but he's the loveliest man,' said Turville. 'Really he is. And it's not really the casino that's upset him, it's because the casino law was passed by the sacred divining rods, by Ora Himself, even though the Council was against it.'

'Oh. How did they do that, then?'

'Well, all the Council's laws come to the Temple, and if Ora doesn't want them to happen then the sacred divining rods glow red, just like they did when they chose you. And the casino thing was the first law that's been changed for thousands of years. It's only natural that it should put the Council's nose out of joint a bit, really.'

Sebastian thought about it. He supposed living in the Temple might be quite interesting if there was a casino, and Mr Meeno was around.

'How about just trying on the sacred robes, Your Knowingness,' said Turville, coaxingly.

The sacred vest and pants were OK. A bit weird, but OK. The sacred socks were nice: black, and not nearly so itchy as his school ones.

'Silk, Your Knowingness. From the worms in the sacred mulberry groves.'

'Oh.' Sebastian tried to imagine how you could train worms to knit socks–perhaps if you tied threads to them they could do it a bit like maypole dancing– but then he abandoned this fascinating idea and hauled on his sacred breeches.

They were the pits–or they would have been, if Sebastian hadn't had to wear the sacred shirt and the sacred robe, as well.

'Very fine, Your Knowingness,' said Turville, tactfully. 'Really impressive.'

'Huh.' Sebastian glowered at himself in the mirror. He'd been right, he did look like a wassail tree. And anyway, there was Gerald to think of. 'Nah,' he said. 'Nice meeting you and all that, but I'm off home, I am.'

'Oh, but, Your Knowingness!' exclaimed Turville. 'Think how much the people need you! Think about how, if you're apprentice, you can have anything you want in the whole world.'

Sebastian halted in the act of pulling off a sacred sock.

'Anything I want?' he echoed. '*Anything?*'

'Oh yes, Your Knowingness. Expense no object. And I like to think I'm quite good about finding suppliers.'

Sebastian considered some more.

'And all I have to do is wear the silly clothes?'

'And receive Offerings when the High Priest isn't here. And have instruction from your tutor, but that's only for an hour a day.'

Sebastian frowned thoughtfully.

'What if I wanted three chocolate éclairs, some super-rambo rat food, a two-metre square nibble-proof cage, twenty feet of metal drainpipe, and a welding kit?'

Turville smiled beatifically.

'They'll be waiting for you as soon as you've finished in the Temple, Your Knowingness. And what shall I order in for your lunch?'

Sebastian paused, and thought. He thought about school, and about his mother's healthy cooking, and about the list of things in his Ambitions Book. About having anything he wanted.

'All right,' he said, at last. 'I'll give it a go as long as Gerald can stay too.'

'Gerald? What a lovely name. And would Gerald be the one who needs the nibble-proof cage, then?'

When Sebastian investigated he found that Gerald was sitting on top of the suitcase cleaning his whiskers. Sebastian picked him up carefully and showed him to Turville. There was no doubt about it: from the tip of his quivering nose to the end of his naked tail, Gerald had class.

Turville thought so, too.

'Ooh,' he said. 'Isn't he handsome?'

Gerald seemed quite happy in his new quarters: he scrabbled about in his sawdust, he ate a sunflower seed, and he began to tear up newspaper in order to make himself a nest.

Turville hadn't stinted on anything. There was a ladder, there was a water-bottle, there was a gold-rimmed bowl for food. Sebastian spent the morning in the crypt with the welding kit and the drainpipe and some special circular guttering Turville had found that had perforations all over the top half.

'So you can see his little furry body scampering about,' said Turville. 'Bless him. Now, what would you fancy for your lunch, Your Knowingness?'

The pizza came with chips and mayonnaise.

'Perfect!' said Sebastian.

'Well, almost,' said Turville. 'Now, ice-cream or treacle pudding? Or something else? You've got plenty of time before Offerings.'

Offerings just meant taking the offering bowl into the Temple whenever the offering bell rang, grabbing whatever people had brought, and scarpering. Oh, and if there was a new baby, you had to say its name, as well.

'Right, thanks a lot,' said Sebastian, as the coins rained

in. 'Yeah, great. Brilliant.'

One of the last people to make an offering that day was a stocky, dark-haired man. He strolled up to the Place of Offering, his hair slicked back and his overcoat hanging magnificently from his broad shoulders and if you hadn't known better, you might easily have made the mistake of thinking he owned the place.

He had some friends with him: a stringy, shifty man who looked as if he had a golf ball wedged in his throat, a huge man who looked like a badly waxed gorilla, and a young woman wearing high heels, a small satin dress, and very heavy eyelashes. The other one was Horace.

It must be Mr Meeno, Sebastian realized, suddenly: Horace's uncle, the gangster. *Wow!*

Everyone made hasty way for them. Mr Meeno and his associates were so famous throughout the City that no one felt they needed to know any more about them.

Mr Meeno arrived at the Place of Offering, looked round consideringly, and raised a hand. The gorilla and the ball-swallower came forward with cloth bags and each poured a stream of coins, glinting and tumbling and chiming as only gold can, into Sebastian's offering bowl.

Everybody in the Temple gasped.

'Cor, ta,' said Sebastian, very impressed. 'Thanks a bundle.'

'See?' hissed Horace, to the dark-haired man. '*Ta, thanks a bundle*? I would have made a miles better apprentice than he does.'

Mr Meeno nodded judiciously, but without taking his sharp black eyes off Sebastian.

'Hey, you, Buster,' he said. 'You in the dress.'

'Hi,' said Sebastian. 'Hey, are you Mr Meeno?'

'Before your very eyes.'

'Cor,' said Sebastian, fervently. 'I've never met a real gangster before.'

The gorilla twitched massively and hauled up a hoarse voice. 'Shall I hit him, boss?'

Mr Meeno put a cigar between his teeth.

'Nah. Show some respect, Jerome. This is the High Priest's apprentice, this is.'

Sebastian smirked.

'Nice to meet you,' he said. '*I'm* going to be a gangster, when I grow up, I am.'

Mr Meeno nodded again.

'That's nice. Ain't that nice, Slats?'

'Sure is, boss,' said the stringy one, through his golf ball.

'But see here, Buster–'

'Sebastian,' said Sebastian. 'Sebastian Blewitt.'

'–just let me give you a bit of what you might specify as career-advice.'

'Cor, really?' said Sebastian, thrilled.

'Yeah. Do you know what I've discovered, in my many

years of successful business enterprise?'

'No,' said Sebastian. 'What?'

'Always deal with the boss. So, no offence, but I need to have a private consultation with the High Priest. Just as a matter of business, you understand.'

Sebastian was extremely disappointed not to be able to help.

'He's gone off on holiday,' he said, regretfully. 'I think he needed to recharge his batteries or something.'

Sebastian found himself on the end of a needle-sharp glance.

'Somehow that does not cause me great surprise,' said Mr Meeno. 'He seemed ill at ease the last time I was with him. So, where is the High Priest on vacation, Mr Apprentice?'

Horace gave a violent and contemptuous sniff.

'He won't know,' he said. 'If *I* was the apprentice I'd be able to find out a thing like that in five minutes.'

Mr Meeno put a hand on Horace's shoulder.

'Sure you could,' he said. 'And I'm sure this young man can do the same. I mean, he looks sharp, doesn't he, Slats?'

Slats allowed his pale little eyes to rest on Sebastian for a second. For him, that was a long time.

'Sure, boss.'

'Sure. In fact, you know, I just wonder if perhaps the

apprentice here might be able to give us any assistance we might need himself.'

Sebastian puffed out his chest.

'Yeah, course,' he said. 'Any time. You just let me know. I mean, seeing as I'm going to be a gangster, myself, I'd like to get some practice and all that.'

'Sure you do,' said Mr Meeno, smoothly. 'And it pleases me more than somewhat to receive such a generous offer.'

Horace tugged urgently at Mr Meeno's sleeve. 'He won't be any help!' he said. 'He'll mess it all up! He'll give us away!'

Mr Meeno patted him on the back.

'Sure, he's only a kid,' he said. 'But you can't rule him out on account of his inches. Why, look at yourself, Horace. No, I've got a feeling I've struck gold here. Hey, kid!'

'Yes, Mr Meeno?'

'I'll be in touch.'

'Course. Yeah. Any time. Just let me know.'

Mr Meeno nodded gently and turned to look at the great golden statue.

'Impressive,' he said. 'Ain't it, Slats?'

Slats's eyes flicked over every wall of the Temple.

'Gives me the creeps, boss.'

'Sure. But, hey, I guess it's a novelty to meet someone

bigger than me. And a god, too. I don't recall ever meeting a god before. Hey, what's-your-name, Ora!'

The echoes of his voice bounced deeply back from the walls, from the floor, from the dome, and became a murmuring part of the Temple. Then there was silence.

Mr Meeno shrugged.

'Well, when He talks, I'm prepared to do business with Him,' he said and he turned and led his company out into the sun.

Chapter 8

Ora was the beginning, and the end, and everything that there was, and is, and shall be.

And in that time, that was not yet time, a tide rose in Ora and He spread out His hand. And lo! There was a mighty tumult and the silence of the universe was ended; and time and space came into being; and they were mighty, and sweet, and beautiful in their perfection.

And Ora dived and spun through the universe that was Himself, and exulted in its glory.

'Did He wear a space helmet?' asked Sebastian.

Mr Walty snorted. 'Don't be silly, Blewitt,' he said, testily; he had been exactly as pleased as Sebastian had been to discover he'd been automatically appointed Sebastian's tutor.

'It's because of continuity,' Turville had explained, comfortingly, placing a big pile of syrupy breakfast pancakes in front of Sebastian.

'Huh,' Sebastian had said and he had meant it.

'Of course He didn't have a space helmet,' snapped Mr Walty.

'But why not?'

Mr Walty tut-tutted.

'Because He didn't need one.'

'Oh. Why not? I mean, He's got nostrils, hasn't He? I mean, you can see right up them on His statue. They look quite small because they're high up, but His hands are huge. So his nostrils must be big so He can get His fingers up them, mustn't they? So if He's got nostrils He must be able to breathe. And if–'

'Ora didn't have nostrils *then*,' said Mr Walty. 'That came later.'

'Ora *grew* nostrils?'

'Yes. I mean, no. He changed form after there were people.'

'Oh. So where did the people come from, then?'

Mr Walty sighed, and turned back to the Sacred Texts.

Time came, and time was, and time passed. The stars and the planets spun, and Ora delighted in the universe that He had called into being.

But then a yearning rose in Ora, and He went to a still, steady place, because the thing He was going to make would not be strong. And He took small strands of the universe that was Himself, and He twisted them together to make a seed, and He planted it. And it began to divide and grow.

'Gerald eats sunflower seeds,' said Sebastian. 'But only if he can't get chocolate and biscuits and stuff.'

'Does he, indeed,' said Mr Walty, drily.

'Yeah,' said Sebastian. 'He's brilliant, Gerald is. Lots of people don't really understand him, though, because he's a rat. But, I mean, Ora must have invented rats, mustn't He?'

'Not exactly, no,' said Mr Walty, and turned back to his book.

The seed grew and it made a perfect circle of greenness on the earth, and Ora saw that it was beautiful. And in His delight He laughed, but Ora's breath was mighty, and it scorched the greenness and withered it, so that it was no longer perfect.

And then Ora fled far away, weeping, diving through the stars, with the new imperfection in the universe quivering throughout His being.

'Talking of being upset,' said Sebastian, 'do you fancy a biscuit?'

Mr Walty snorted.

'For goodness' sake concentrate, boy! What on earth has the creation of life got to do with biscuits?'

'Because when people are upset, that's what they do,' he said. 'Eat biscuits. It's brilliant, here. Turville can get you any sort of biscuit you want, even if it's something like walnut and raspberry crunch with caramel topping.'

'Oh,' said Mr Walty, thrown off track. 'Really? I didn't know they did them with caramel topping.'

'Neither did I. Turville!'

Turville was in his dusting apron, but he was more than happy to bring them a plate full of more kinds of biscuits than Sebastian had ever seen in his life.

'Brilliant,' said Sebastian, through a liquorice cream.

'Really splendid, Turville,' said Mr Walty. 'Such a change from the school staffroom. Quite marvellous. Now, where were we?'

Mr Walty cleared the crumbs from his throat and began to read again.

After many years Ora's sorrow was spent, and He returned to purify that place. But lo! He found there a great garden, full of diverse flowers and mighty trees. And Ora perceived that the harm He had done to the seed had changed it, so that sometimes a new generation was different from that from which it had sprung. And Ora wandered for a long time in the garden, entranced and full of pleasure; for although the garden was not perfect, being full of death and decay, still it was beautiful and it fascinated Him.

Turville came in with Sebastian's sacred boots.

'I'm terribly sorry to disturb you, but the limo's here,' he announced. 'We've just got time to get to the model train shop before Offerings, Your Knowingness.'

Mr Walty took a last swig at his tea.

'Well, we've got some work done, I suppose,' he said,

grudgingly. 'And I must be getting back to school. I'll see you tomorrow, Blewitt. Half-past ten.'

Sebastian settled back happily into the reconstructed limo and waved to the small crowd of tourists gathered outside. There were two other people outside the Temple, but no one was taking any notice of them. One was a man with his hat pulled down over his eyes, who was taking photographs of everyone who went into the Temple; and the other was Finley Wortle. He was wearing a sandwich board.

It said: 'ORA IS DEAD.'

Chapter 9

Sebastian went home on Tuesday evening to a warm welcome from Mr and Mrs Blewitt. Edward and Robert and Eunice were rather cooler.

'It was *such* a thrill to see you in your robes in the Temple,' said Mrs Blewitt, dewy-eyed. 'Did you see us, Sebastian? I painted myself an 'Apprentice's Mother' T-shirt. Oh, we were so proud! Weren't we, Robert?'

'More terminally embarrassed, actually,' said Robert, in a growl.

'He wasn't exactly impressive, was he?' pointed out Edward, thin-lipped.

'Oh, but I thought he looked so dignified in his lovely robe.'

'Dignified?' snapped Eunice. 'When he mooches in with his hands in his pockets, mutters "What yerwant?" and "Oh. All right. Ta" before snatching the offerings and walking off? No one could call that dignified. Not in a hundred years.'

'Yeah,' said Sebastian, patiently, 'but then I don't have to be dignified, do I? All I have to do is get the offerings. So I don't have to bother about being dignified, do I? I mean, do I?'

Mr and Mrs Blewitt exchanged glances.

'Well,' began Mr Blewitt, carefully.

'I mean, it's called having character,' pointed out Sebastian, warming to his theme. 'No one wants some boring old person who just comes on and does the same old thing, do they?'

'Well,' said Mrs Blewitt, wrinkling her forehead.

'No. They want character. They want entertainment, don't they?'

Mr Blewitt stroked his beard rather nervously.

'So,' went on Sebastian, his eyes brightening as possibilities opened in front of him, 'I thought that I'd work out a few routines.'

'Great Ora!' exclaimed Robert. 'He's going to do a song and dance!'

Sebastian considered this. *Yeah. Perhaps if Turville got him a stick with a knob on the end–and he came down the stairs sort of sideways – and if Turville got him some tap-dancing shoes ... Yeah.*

'And I thought,' he went on, 'that sometimes I could swing in on a rope, sort of like a gibbon, going "Oh-er-oh-er-oh-er," you know. Or, on special occasions, I could fly in like they do in the Wassail Plays, on an invisible wire.'

Eunice gave a hollow laugh.

'Or you could parachute in from the dome,' she said.

'Cor!' said Sebastian. 'Yeah!'

'Eunice!' said Mrs Blewitt. 'Don't encourage him!'

Sebastian looked at his mother, deeply wounded.

'But you're meant to encourage me,' he said. 'Here I am, trying to be *creative*, and you –'

Mrs Blewitt went a little pink and flustered. 'But, Sebastian –'

Sebastian got to his feet. 'I think I'll just go to my room for a little while,' he said. 'To be quiet.'

Mr and Mrs Blewitt exchanged looks of alarm.

'Are you all right?' asked Mr Blewitt.

Sebastian passed a weary hand across his forehead.

'I think so,' he said, still more bravely. 'Just a bit tired. All these new things to learn – it can make you a bit exhausted, to begin with.'

He sucked in his cheeks pathetically and trailed out. Mrs Blewitt was saying something to the others about needing to be tremendously supportive. Sebastian smirked, went to his room, and wrote *Do a parachute jump* in his Ambitions Book.

Gerald was pleased to see Sebastian on his return to the Temple.

'Did Turville look after you all right?' asked Sebastian, scratching Gerald behind the ear.

'Indeed I did, Your Knowingness. I gave him that cornflake packet that was nearly empty and he had a lovely time rummaging about. Oh, and I phoned the military, and you have to do a training course before your parachute jump, and they were asking when you'd like to do it.'

'Tomorrow, after Offerings,' said Sebastian. 'Do you think I could go in a proper army jeep?'

'It'll be at the door at three o'clock, Your Knowingness. Oh, and Councillor Kimber is waiting for you in the schoolroom to get some laws ratified.'

'Get them what?'

'Oh, just sort of agreed by Ora and the Temple. You just have to wave the sacred divining rods over them, and if the ends don't glow red then they're the will of Ora, bless His holy name. Nothing to worry about.'

Councillor Kimber had a briefcase handcuffed to his wrist.

'Ah, apprentice,' he said, and twiddled the combination locks. 'Normally this is the High Priest's duty, but fortunately the law allows for you to stand in for him. So if you'll just pass the rods over these.'

The new laws covered a whole wad of thick cream paper. Sebastian peered at the top sheet, but the writing was curly and the words were long.

Turville trotted in with the sacred divining rods on a velvet cushion. Sebastian picked them up curiously. They felt oddly unbalanced and uncontrollable in his hands.

'Right,' said Councillor Kimber, checking his watch. 'If you'll just perform the rite, apprentice, then I can get on. Yes, that's quite adequate, apprentice, we don't want to put anyone's eye out.'

Sebastian peered at the little spheres.

'What if they'd lit up?' asked Sebastian.

Councillor Kimber was already gathering up the papers, knocking them briskly back into a neat block, and then putting them back into his briefcase.

'I don't think we need worry about that,' he said. 'As far as we know it's only happened once.'

'Ooh,' said Turville. 'And that's a day I'll never forget. You could have knocked me right down with a feather. And the High Priest, he was in such a doodah, just running with perspiration, poor man. All that trouble and caused just by this new casino. Well, the wisdom of Ora works in mysterious ways.'

'Mysterious indeed,' said Councillor Kimber, with a scowl.

He gave the smallest, most formal bow, and made for the door. Turville was only just in time to open it for him.

'There,' said Turville. 'That's that. Always lovely to see him, but he never hangs about, does Councillor Kimber. Always busy-busy. Not a chatty type at all. Never was. Now, give me back those rods, there's a sweetheart, and I'll put them back in the Treasury.'

'Cor! Is there a Treasury?'

'Oh yes, of course there is. The key's on the hook by the loo door, if you ever need to get in. Hasn't got that much in it, really – just stuff for the Temple, like the best offering bowl and the High Priest's Robes for Special Occasions.'

'Like Turkey Day and Wassail?'

'That's right, Your Knowingness.'

Sebastian frowned.

'But really, coming to the Temple is always special, isn't it?' he said. 'So I was thinking, we ought to make it special, oughtn't we? I mean, Mr Meeno or someone might come.'

'Special?' asked Turville, batting his beautiful eyelashes.

'Yeah. I thought we could get in a band, and have dancing and stuff.'

Turville looked at his watch.

'Well, there's only a couple of hours until Offerings, but we could probably manage a three-piece jazz combo. As for the dancers –'

'Oh, that's all right. We just need a gold walking stick and some tap shoes. And a hooter.'

'A hooter and some tap shoes, Your Knowingness?'

'Yeah. Size six.'

Chapter 10

'Does everyone know what they're doing?' asked Sebastian, as he shrugged himself into his sacred Offerings cloak.

'Oh yes, Your Knowingness. We've set the band up in front of the High Priest's chair. As soon as you honk the hooter they'll start to play.'

'That's right,' said Sebastian. 'And then I'll come down the steps sort of sideways, with my stick in my hand, and when I stretch my arms out and go "Yeah!" the piano has to do a sort of jangling thing until the drum bangs the lid on it. OK?'

'All arranged, Your Knowingness. And I'm sure it's going to be wonderful. Such a treat for everybody. And such a surprise.'

People *were* surprised. They were frozen with it: from the moment Sebastian squeezed the rubber bulb on the hooter everyone was completely riveted. All Sebastian could see, when he sneaked a glance round the High Priest's throne and through the drum kit, was an assembly of wax figures with wide open eyes and mouths. Sebastian waited for the echoes to stop dodging about through the pillars and signalled to the band.

It was a good band. They were a bit wrinkly, and their polo necks bulged over their paunches a bit, but they had style. They had pizzazz. Sebastian grasped his stick and launched himself, arms outspread, into his grand entrance.

Actually, tap shoes weren't the best things to wear if you were doing high kicks all the way down a flight of stairs. Still, he didn't fall over, and the twirly things he had been practising with his stick made everyone gasp. And when he bounced the stick so it boinged back into his hand on its secret bit of elastic, several people cheered.

The mustard-gowned vergers were even more surprised than everybody else. They were so surprised they didn't even join in the round of applause and cheerful hooting from the rest of the congregation; they were so surprised they didn't even look as if they'd enjoyed it.

But so much money went into the offering bowl that they had to bring in the special-occasion one from the Treasury to take the overspill.

Sebastian was pleased to see that a sharp-suited figure with a pulled-down hat had witnessed the whole thing.

He trusted the man would go back to Mr Meeno and tell him all about it.

Chapter 11

The parachute course was brilliant. Sebastian was allowed to do the training course with a platoon of real soldiers. You had to jump off things and fall over. The class was taught by a cockerel-strutting sergeant who grew great bulging veins in his neck when he bellowed, and it was all fantastic, especially the roaring. You had to roar when you hit the ground.

The sergeant loved him.

'Listen to that young lad, there, you weak-lunged, pink-livered, knock-kneed bunch of ... of *daffodils*!' he hissed, for he always seemed to be trying to shout as loudly as he could without actually opening his teeth. 'There's a roar for you: put the fear of Ora, bless His holy name, into anyone, that would! The rest of you sound like a load of sore-throated gerbils in tight collars!'

Sebastian climbed into the back of the jeep at the end of the training session quite blissfully happy, and Mr Walty, whose job it had been to accompany him, heaved himself up with a grunt beside him.

'You're not cold, are you?' asked Sebastian, because Mr Walty was all twitchy and shivery.

Mr Walty raised a green face.

'No, no. Just a little ... shocked.'

'It was exciting, wasn't it?' said Sebastian, as the sentries saluted and the high security gates slid open before them.

Mr Walty gave a laugh that sounded as if it came from the dome of the Temple.

'When the straps of your harness snapped and you nearly dropped twenty feet onto concrete?' he said. 'Yes, that certainly relieved the tedium, Blewitt.'

'Yeah, I liked that bit,' said Sebastian, because it'd been quite interesting to hang there from one arm and watch thirty grown-ups stampeding over to form a pyramid to rescue him and it'd been quite something to see the sergeant going all putty-coloured and calm with embarrassment over the frayed harness. 'You know, I think acrobats would be quite good in the Temple,' he said, thoughtfully. 'In shiny gold suits and stuff.'

They were nearly onto the public road now. Sebastian was waving a cheery goodbye to the last set of saluting guards when he noticed that there was someone skulking amongst the bushes by the side of the road. It looked a bit small for a soldier. In fact, it looked just like Horace Meeno.

But it couldn't be Horace. Of course not, not on a school day. Horace would have been stuck inside all day with Dora and all that lot.

At that thought Sebastian found himself filled with a

sense of great good fortune.

'This is a lot better than being at school,' he said. And at that Mr Walty sighed, and leant back against the canvas side of the jeep.

'Tuesday afternoon,' he mused. 'Double Derek Parrot and Form 9G. The most determinedly ignorant and malodorous set of juveniles on the planet.'

He blew out a long breath and for once he even stopped scowling. 'Much better, Blewitt,' he said.

The sergeant had reckoned the dome wasn't high enough for a parachute jump, but he'd suggested using a zip-wire, instead. That was probably a good idea, because then Sebastian wouldn't have to worry about landing on somebody's great-aunt. Mind you, that would have livened things up a bit.

Sebastian leant back against one of Ora's great ankles and gazed thoughtfully round at the gloom of the Temple. It felt quite different in the Temple at night, without the whole place being filled with glossy-shoed vergers and proud clattering families.

It wasn't peaceful at all in here in the daytime: people were too busy *doing* things to be peaceful. Mrs Poash had been moaning like mad only that afternoon because she'd discovered a boy in the Temple with a toy pistol. She'd scolded the boy thoroughly, dragged him off by the ear, and then come and sniffed at Sebastian, as if it was his fault.

'Children!' she'd said, with the crispest loathing and loftiest hauteur. 'They have no sense of the dignity of the Temple, the little wretches. They should be kept at home, under control.'

And it was certainly true that the boy with the pistol had been extremely ugly. In fact, from where Sebastian had been standing, it'd looked quite like Horace Meeno.

Sebastian wondered if he was going bonkers: he was seeing Horace everywhere. Yuck.

Beams of light bounced off the statue of Ora and cartwheeled away along gold-veined tiles to make the pillars glow.

'Nice place you've got here,' said Sebastian.

'Your Knowingness!'

Turville's voice came to him clearly from somewhere across the darkness. 'Supper's on the table, Your Knowingness, just as you ordered.'

'Coming,' called Sebastian, scrambling to his feet.

The chill of the Temple struck him the moment he stepped outside the pool of light surrounding the statue. He paused for a second, looking up over his shoulder at the great tiger-stone eyes that seemed black and deep in the dimness of the statue's fine brows.

'See you, OK?' he muttered and made his way back to his rooms.

Turville's popcorn and marmalade pizza was brilliant.

'Well, it does make a change,' said Turville, cutting Sebastian his third helping. 'His last Knowingness wasn't what you'd call creative about food. Scrambled eggs on toast, he had, every single day, with a cup of tea, no sugar.'

'Every day? When he could have had anything he wanted?'

'That's right. Still, he was happy, and that's the main thing.'

Sebastian offered Gerald a piece of popcorn. Gerald was mad on popcorn.

'What was he called?' Sebastian asked.

'Cyril. Yes, Cyril. A lovely boy. One of the most *intellectual* apprentices we've seen for many a long year. Why, even Mrs Poash liked him, poor dear. Yes. I was very sorry to see him go.'

'He went early, didn't he? To the university.'

'That's right, Your Knowingness. Writing a dissertation on the gold vaults he is, bless him. Still, he's very happy there. I'm afraid he got very anxious, towards the end, what with all this fuss about the sacred divining rods changing the casino law, and then that time when he nearly got electrocuted after the toaster somehow managed to fall into his bath. Still,' Turville went on, with a sigh, 'it's all part of life, and that's something we can't get away from. Even Ora, bless His holy name, can't make everything perfect.'

'Can't he?'

Turville stared at him.

'Well, no, of course not, Your Knowingness,' he said. 'Otherwise He'd have done it, wouldn't He?'

Chapter 12

One day Ora was sitting in the shade of a great tree when He felt a sharp unpleasantness in part of Himself; and He perceived a tiny thing with a body of black and yellow stripes sitting on Him; and Ora was so astonished that He sat and watched the thing until it had finished cleaning its feelers and had flown away.

'I bet that was a wasp,' said Sebastian. 'I got stung by a wasp, once. And I was only trying to find out how furry it was. Or it could have been a bee, I suppose.'

'If you'll stop interrupting, perhaps we'll find out,' said Mr Walty, testily, turning a page.

And Ora went with the tiny thing until they came to a whole city of similar creatures, all living with their lives intertwined; and at the heart of the city was a hoard of soft gold. And Ora spoke to the creature, and He said, 'Why did you cause me that unpleasantness?' But the creature made no answer.

And then, as if He had been stung to the heart, Ora knew that He was alone in all the Universe.

And He wept.

Mrs Poash was always first into the Temple in the mornings. Sebastian, high on the walkway that encircled the dome, sometimes looked down on her shining silver hair as she stood before the golden statue.

Quite often, she wept, too.

Chapter 13

And Ora left the earth, and swam through the universe, calling; and although the infinity of time and space was perfect, there was nothing that could answer Him, not in the icefields of the moon, nor in the fierce flames of the sun.

'I wouldn't like it if I hadn't got Gerald to talk to,' said Sebastian, thoughtfully.

'Or your family,' suggested Mr Walty.

'Huh,' said Sebastian. 'You've never tried living with them.'

And after Ora had called out His great aloneness through all the universe, He went back to the place of the treasure-beast: but lo! It was gone, and in its place was a medium-sized blobby creature.

And Ora spoke to the creature, and He said, 'Who are you?'

But the creature was overcome by the glory of Ora, and it screamed in mighty fear and fled into a hole in the ground. But Ora wished to know more of the creature, and so He made Himself small and followed the creature into the earth, and there He found it trembling and telling several other blobby creatures about the great waterfall that had spoken to him with a voice of thunder.

'I bet they were people,' said Sebastian. 'The High Priest, he's really blobby, like a jelly baby, he is. Only older, and bulgier, of course. More like a jelly hippopotamus, really.'

'Oh good grief,' said Mr Walty.

And then the others all shook in mighty terror as well.

And Ora pitied their terror, and He made Himself the same size and shape as the others, only perfectly beautiful.

And then the creatures were much amazed, and the hairiest one said, 'What are you doing here?'

And Ora answered them in their own language, and He said: 'I have come to live among you.'

And at that the creatures were greatly troubled; and after some conference amongst themselves, the hairiest one spoke again, and he said: 'Just who do you think you are?'

And Ora smiled upon him, and He said: 'My name is Ora, and I am God.'

After Offerings that afternoon Sebastian found a man in a square smart suit waiting for him by the door to his rooms.

'Hey,' the man said.

Sebastian put down his flashing hula-hoop, his party blowers, and his pair of maracas.

'Are you one of Mr Meeno's friends?' he asked, admiringly, taking in the man's square neck and long, tasteful scar.

'Harry,' answered the man. 'Sometimes they call me Harry the Hangman on account of my great interest in ropes and such. Mr Meeno, he wanted me to tell you he's impressed.'

'Coo,' said Sebastian, delighted. 'Really?'

'Yeah. Yeah. With the trampolining choir, and the bunny impersonators, and the whole caboodle. He says it's a sign of considerable talent and genius.'

'Huh,' said a shadow that slid greasily out from behind a pillar. 'Well, I've been at school with him and I say he's a dummy.'

'Is that so?' asked Harry. 'Well, I guess you would be the expert as regards dummies. But, hey, Mr Apprentice, Mr Meeno, he has what you might call a proposition. He wanted me to point out that every business, even a well-run one like Meeno Inc., runs into what you might call sticky situations. Situations where a little inside help might prove a considerable advantage.'

'Don't trust him!' spat Horace, spitefully.

'And Mr Meeno, he was wondering if there might be anything you were in need of,' went on Harry, ignoring him. 'Because Mr Meeno is a generous man, and he's really what you might say taken you to his heart. He'd like to give you the benefit of his experience.'

Sebastian was immensely flattered.

'That's really kind of Mr Meeno,' he said. 'But, the thing is, I can have anything I like, anyway, what with me being apprentice and all that. So I'm all right, thanks.'

'See?' said Horace. 'I told you he wouldn't be interested.'

Harry grunted and scowled.

'Mr Meeno,' he said, dangerously, 'he's a powerful man. No one would want to get on the wrong side of him.'

'Yeah,' said Sebastian. 'I know. He's incredible, Mr Meeno is. That's why I want to be a gangster, too, just like him. Me and Gerald. I want to run my own business, you see, and not have people telling me what to do.'

Harry's face darkened still further.

'I think I should inform you that being a gangster is a very dangerous game,' he said. 'People who get in the way have to be shifted, if you get my meaning.'

'Yes,' said Sebastian, happily. 'Being a gangster is the best thing ever. Tell Mr Meeno thanks for the offer, all right?'

Sebastian took Gerald for a tour of the Temple that evening. Gerald was quite interested, and thoroughly enjoyed climbing through the stone tree-tracery above the High Priest's throne.

'It's good, isn't it,' said Sebastian, to Turville, when Turville came to say his double-decker cheeseburger with no salad had arrived. 'But I don't think there are any carved rats anywhere. There are loads of bees and turkeys, but not a single rat.'

'You know, I think you might be right,' said Turville. 'I expect it's because rats have never been a written-down part of the story of Ora. All the carvings and paintings tell bits of His story.'

'Well, they're part of the story of Ora and the Temple now,' said Sebastian, firmly.

Gerald must have caught the scent of the burger, because his neat nose was quivering and his whiskers were sprung with excitement and intelligence. Sebastian put Gerald down on the gold-patterned floor and Gerald made for Sebastian's quarters in a determined keyboard-patter of sharp claws.

'He knows his way all round the Temple already,' said Sebastian, proudly. 'Even though I've only shown him once.'

Gerald's trundling shadow ticked across the aisle, rattled along under a row of chairs, and pattered down past the huge bank of speakers Sebastian had had brought in to provide a bit of atmosphere on the jazz band's days off.

Halfway along the wall of speakers Gerald squeaked sharply and seemed to rebound from something.

'Hey, what's up with Gerald?' asked Sebastian, in concern, as Gerald did a frantic somersaulting squirm, righted himself, and then streaked for the door to their quarters like a stream of jet-powered smoke.

But there was a sudden inexplicable readjustment of the shadows in the space in front of him as he spoke – a faint musty draught – and then a

BOOM-OOM-OOOOOM! the hugest and most appalling sound ever and for a moment Sebastian thought the dome had fallen in, and most of the sky with it.

It was a long time before the noise lessened to no more than the buzzing of his ears and the galloping of his heart. A heaving *whoomph* of dust blew a million grains of incense-tinged mildew all over the two of them.

'Cor!' said Sebastian, hugely surprised and very impressed. 'What –'

'The speakers, Your Knowingness,' said Turville, rather breathlessly. 'Those great big speakers. Look, every one of them's come right down.'

They had to go round through the vergers' vestry to view the damage. The four monumental speakers in their cases of rock-hard oak had toppled across the aisle and smashed onto the cupboards that held the vergers' wassail hats.

Sebastian whistled. Everything was crushed down to four feet high, with ragged splinters of wood and ripped pieces of cloth-of-gold jutting jaggedly up at the dust-sinking dome.

'That could have been dangerous,' said Sebastian, a bit shocked. 'If that'd been anyone but Gerald walking under there, they'd have had their heads bashed in.'

Turville drew in a long but unsteady breath.

'Thank goodness it was Gerald, then,' he said. 'And those horrid wassail hat cupboards. I never did like them. Quite wrong for the Temple, all that nasty dark mahogany.'

'Yeah. Yeah. Look, I'd better go and find Gerald, hadn't I. Let him know everything's all right.'

'You do that, Your Knowingness. The poor little thing must have jumped halfway out of his skin.'

Turville stayed behind for a little while, quietly, his fair head bowed as if in thought. Then he bent down and took up a thin dark wire that protruded from under one of the ruined speakers. He followed it, carefully, back to the place where it had been secured to trip an unwary ankle. The speakers must have been pushed forward on their plinths right to toppling point, so that the smallest tug on the wire had set them falling. Turville sighed, untwisted the wire, and put it away in his pocket.

Gerald was cowering sawdustily in the bottom of his cage. Sebastian sat with him for a little while and explained what had happened. Sebastian stroked Gerald, first with a finger, and then properly, but when Sebastian finally picked him up he could feel the frantic ticking of Gerald's panic-stricken heart. Sebastian waited until Gerald was a bit quieter, and then they shared the cheeseburger.

Sebastian kept Gerald with him all evening, and soon Gerald was happy to investigate the new table train-layout Sebastian had got for passing the salt and sugar at meal times. And when Sebastian came back from asking Turville about an extension lead, Gerald had gone. That was all right. It just meant that old Gerald had caught the whiff of something interesting and had gone exploring.

But Turville was a bit worried about it.

'This is a very old place, Your Knowingness,' he said. 'And there are all sorts of things that it might not be good for Gerald to explore.'

'Are there?' asked Sebastian, intrigued. 'Like what?'

But Turville only went vague.

'The Temple's been here for more than a thousand years,' he said. 'And there were other Temples here before that. You never know what a rat, an intelligent, inquisitive rat like Gerald, might sniff out.'

Sebastian considered.

'Gerald did bite through the telephone wire at home, once,' he said. 'It took the telephone people three days to find out what was wrong. They had half the street up. Cor, and they weren't half wild when they found out!'

'Well, there we are,' said Turville, tossing back his hair dramatically. 'Think of that, Your Knowingness: if that poor little creature were to find one of the main power lines ... ooh, I can't bear to think about it.'

'Would it make his whiskers go curly?' asked Sebastian. He didn't have much time for fancy rats, as a rule, but he'd often wondered if curly whiskers really worked.

But Turville only shook his head, really distressed.

'It'd do more than that, Your Knowingness, the poor little thing. Roast him, it would, poor sweetheart. To just a poor little mound of charred –'

But Sebastian had gone.

Sebastian found Gerald licking up a scattering of biscuit crumbs in the passage. Sebastian waited until Gerald had finished, and then picked him up carefully.

'Perhaps you'd better stay in your run unless I'm around to look after you,' said Sebastian.

Gerald whiffled his whiskers and looked reproachful.

'Yeah, yeah, I know, I know,' said Sebastian. 'But Turville says it might be dangerous.'

Gerald gave him a filthy look, and Sebastian, sighing,

had to admit he had a point.

'Look,' he said, 'I'll tell you what we'll do. We'll go out into the Temple every day, right, until we've explored everywhere really properly. And once we've done that, and we've worked out where the really dangerous bits are, then you can go about by yourself. And I'll tell you what,' he went on, hurriedly, as Gerald seemed about to raise an invisible but withering eyebrow, 'we'll go and explore the Treasury now, straight away, OK?'

The key was on the hook by the loo door, just as Turville had said. The Treasury door looked just like any other door: in fact, it could easily have been a broom cupboard.

'Cunning, huh?' said Sebastian, as he put the key in the lock. 'No one would think of looking in here. Safe as houses, this must be.'

Sebastian felt for the light switch and flicked it on. The Treasury very nearly *was* a broom cupboard. The best offering bowl was there on a shelf, but it wasn't half as big or splendid as the everyday one, even though the everyday one was only gold-plated. There was a clothes rail with a whole load of robes on it, but though they were encrusted with barnacles and carbuncles of gold lace and embroidery they somehow still had a forlorn, junk-shop look about them.

And that was nearly all there was. Sebastian looked

round, a bit puzzled. You couldn't go three steps in the Temple without tripping over a work of golden art, and so it was unbelievable that the Temple Treasury should be so small and sparse and ... and tacky. It was especially puzzling when you remembered all the bowlfuls of offerings that rained into the Temple every day of the year. What happened to them? Well, they must go down to the gold vaults somehow, Sebastian supposed.

Gerald was thinking about trying the jump from Sebastian's shoulder to the shelf that held the best offering bowl, so Sebastian held up his arm so he could get there more easily. Gerald clawed his way carefully down Sebastian's sleeve and had a good sniff round. The only other thing on the shelf, apart from a set of little tasselled wassail bells, was a familiar golden box. Sebastian opened it, and picked out one of the divining rods. The gold was satisfyingly heavy, and left a trace of mist when he ran his thumb along the silky smoothness of the shaft.

Gerald was investigating the other rod. He whiffled his whiskers along from one end of the thing to the other, flicking the thing delicately with his tongue. Then he had a go at biting the end off.

Sebastian hastily retrieved the rod.

'Don't eat that,' he said. 'That's a sacred divining rod, that is. Probably poisonous. Neat though, isn't it, being gold, and all? Clever, too, knowing to choose us.'

Sebastian made sure Gerald hadn't left any teeth marks. There was just a faint line where the gold shone a paler colour, but a quick polish would probably rub it out.

Sebastian rubbed the place determinedly with his thumb.

And the sphere at the other end glowed red.

Sebastian nearly dropped it.

Why had that happened? Because it had been pointing at his belly-button?

Or because –

Sebastian had to look very, very carefully before he found the place where one piece of the shaft joined the other. If you pushed at it in just the right way a piece of metal slid open to reveal–

A battery.

A battery?

Now Sebastian knew what to look for, he could see that the golden sphere on the end of the divining rod was not solid gold at all, but glass, covered with a sheet of gold leaf as thin as breath. It was so thin that the red bulb inside shone through when you squeezed the rods to join the connections inside.

Sebastian weighed them in his hands and he wondered. He wondered about the High Priest, in whose hands the divining rods had rejected one of the Council's laws for the first time ever; and he also wondered for the first time why it had been he who had been chosen as the High Priest's apprentice.

Sebastian put the rods back as he had found them and went to bed.

Chapter 14

The parachute jump was brilliant. Sebastian took his certificate home on Saturday, and Robert was pleasingly jealous.

The dome had proved, as expected, not high enough for a parachute drop, but the Field Marshal that Turville consulted had known all about zip-wires.

'Brilliant,' said Sebastian. 'Will you get some people in to set it all up? I thought I could come down from the Muttering Gallery in a sort of swirl.'

Turville raised a beautifully-shaped eyebrow.

'And what will the harness do to your sacred robe?' he asked. 'I suppose you'll be wanting me to sew on shoulder pads, next, to stop it chafing.'

'Yeah,' said Sebastian, happily. 'That'd be brilliant. Can they be really big ones, like horse-wrestlers wear?'

Turville shook his head, but he was smiling.

'You'll have the vergers muttering and grumping. They haven't got used to the limbo dancers, yet. Mrs Poash has been going on something alarming, bless her.'

'Yeah, I know,' said Sebastian. 'But Mrs Poash and the vergers like muttering and grumping: it's what keeps them going.'

Turville laughed.

'But I'm still not sure about your coming down a zip-wire in your robe,' he said. 'You might get your skirts in a tangle. Ooh, and you'll get terribly creased!'

Sebastian thought about it.

'You could make some slits in the skirts,' he suggested.

'Make some slits? In your sacred robe?'

'Yeah,' said Sebastian. 'Up the sides. Hey, do you think you could get it done by tomorrow, because it'd be great if the wire was up by then. Oh, and I'd like to go for a trip on the footplate of a steam train this afternoon, after Offerings.'

'Whatever you say, Your Knowingness,' said Turville, but his tone was tart.

'Now,' said Mr Walty, 'we were studying Ora's creation of life. Can you remember where we'd got to?'

'Ora had just gone to live with the blobby people,' said Sebastian.

'The what?'

'You know,' said Sebastian. 'The cave men.'

'Humph. Well, the next bit of the story explains why there's always an apprentice in the Temple.'

'Oh, right. Hang on, here's Turville with the biscuits.'

'Bit flouncy today, isn't he?' observed Mr Walty, when Turville had gone.

'Yeah. Don't know why, unless he's upset because

I'm going to ride on the footplate of a steam engine this afternoon. Tell you what, I'll invite him along. That'll cheer him up.'

So Ora dwelt among them, and everything was nearly perfect. They lived a life of ease and pleasure; and sometimes they would even try to answer the questions that Ora asked. The little ones were best at this, because their heads were less cluttered up with the things of the world. The little ones were also not so worried by the fact that Ora could appear and disappear whenever He pleased, so that no one ever knew where on earth He was going to turn up next. The little ones would cheer whenever they saw Ora, and run to Him, and clamber all over Him, and chatter and play catch with Him; but the big ones would bow, and keep their eyes on the ground, and they never asked Him fishing.

'Oh, right,' said Sebastian. 'Ora chooses an apprentice to live with Him in the Temple because grown-ups are all really boring.'

'I prefer to think of it as a sign of His infinite patience,' said Mr Walty, drily.

But one day a young man went fishing and did not return; and all the people, both big and small, were full of fear.

But Ora went to the young man, and pulled him from the deep mud by the river, and he was saved.

And it so happened that later that day a young woman came to Ora, and she knelt before Him, and she made Him an offering of a shiny stone the colour of honey.

And Ora understood that it contained her love for Him; and He kept it, and it gave Him great joy.

Turville declined the opportunity to ride on the steam train.

'Too busy doing your alterations, that's what I am,' he sniffed.

'Oh,' said Sebastian. 'Well – look, it doesn't really matter if it isn't done today. I mean, it's not desperate or anything.'

Turville looked up from where he was stabbing a shining needle through the thick layers of sacred robe, and his eyes went suddenly as warm as teacakes.

'Oh, don't worry,' he said. 'I don't mind, not really. Glad of a chance to put my feet up, after a whole hour of listening to people complaining.'

'Mrs Poash again?'

'Oh, dear Mrs Poash. Ooh, I do love her so much. Such a dedicated, committed lady. Poor thing.'

'Poor thing?'

'Oh yes, it's a very sad story. But never mind that now,

Your Knowingness. Off you go and have a good time.'

Sebastian had a glorious time, and he had his photograph taken between the driver and the fireman.

'Oh dear,' said Mrs Blewitt. 'Didn't anyone *tell* you that your face was so dirty?'

'You look a complete idiot, grinning all over your face like that,' said Edward, his face sour with envy.

Sebastian smirked, and went up to his bedroom to make a tick against another entry in his Ambitions Book. There weren't that many ambitions left unticked, now, and it was the wrong season for frogspawn, but it gave Sebastian an idea. He got Turville to get him a catalogue of all the crawliest sorts of animals you could buy and he spent ages wavering between toxic-toed toads, venomous vine-frogs, and strangler snakes. In the end Turville, a little haggard, suggested a guided tour of the Reptile House at the zoo.

That was brilliant, too, though after a long talk to the Head Keeper, Sebastian regretfully came to the conclusion he hadn't time to look after any more pets and anyway, Gerald was all he needed. But the Head Keeper said that Sebastian was welcome at the Reptile House any time, and he was allowed to hold a python.

Eunice introduced a new sour note.

'What's happening about the casino?' she asked. 'They're saying that apparently there's nothing anyone can do to stop it unless the High Priest decides he was wrong about it all. The papers are screaming.'

'The papers are always screaming about something,' said Edward, sounding ancient and weary.

'Yes,' said Eunice, 'but this really is important. This is the first time the sacred divining rods have thrown out one of the Council's laws for at least a thousand years. And over a silly thing like building a casino on the Holy Hill!'

'A casino sounds a good idea, to me,' said Sebastian. 'I reckon people will enjoy it. Anyway, it'll give me somewhere to go in the evening.'

'You wouldn't be allowed in. Children aren't.'

'No, but I would be.'

'No you wouldn't.'

'Oh yes I would,' said Sebastian, patiently. 'I mean, I was allowed to do a parachute jump, wasn't I, and children aren't allowed. And I was allowed to ride on the footplate of a steam engine; and I was allowed to sit in the director's box to watch the International; and I was allowed to hold a python. Wasn't I? Well, wasn't I?'

'They were probably hoping it would strangle you,' said Robert, darkly.

'Oh no they weren't. If they didn't like me they wouldn't have asked me back, would they? They wouldn't have said I was welcome any time. They wouldn't have said how good I was at holding a python. Or–'

'No,' said Mrs Blewitt, soothingly. 'I'm sure they wouldn't have, Sebastian, dear. But I'm afraid a casino will be rather out of place. Your father says it'll be just where the tourists congregate.'

'Well, there you are, then,' said Sebastian. 'I mean, there'll be all those people wandering up and down with nothing to do except look at Finley Wortle and his sandwich board, or all those boring old buildings. And then they'll see the casino, and they'll think how nice it would be to have a sit down and do something interesting.'

'I can't believe this,' said Eunice, rolling her eyes.

'I mean, we're supposed to make the tourists happy, aren't we?' demanded Sebastian. 'I mean, they won't come unless they're happy, will they? And so why shouldn't they have a nice casino as a change from having to trudge round all those boring buildings all the time?'

Eunice ran her hands through her fair hair.

'I just cannot comprehend how anyone can be so moronic,' she said. 'Don't you understand how dangerous things are? People don't much like the Temple having anything to do with ruling the City as it is. But now the High Priest's actually changed a law, then anything could happen. The papers are howling, and the Council's furious. We may be headed for a revolution!'

'Really?' said Sebastian. 'Cool!'

Eunice lifted her hands beseechingly.

'See?' she said. 'Moronic. Totally stupid.'

'Sebastian isn't stupid, darling,' said Mrs Blewitt. 'He's just very ... er ... original.'

Eunice snorted.

'Yes, and I bet the High Priest was very original when he consulted the Sacred Texts over the casino law,' she said.

'Really, Eunice!' Mrs Blewitt was quite shocked. 'What a dreadful idea. The thought of the High Priest misreading the Sacred Texts so he could get laws passed! I'm sure the High Priest's never *dreamed* of doing anything of the sort.'

'Anyway, he can't have planned it,' pointed out Edward, seriously. 'You can't get away from the fact that the sacred divining rods glowed red just when the laws about building on the Holy Hill were going through. I mean, that was a *miracle*. That was the voice of *Ora*.'

Sebastian took a large bite at his slice of wholemeal bread, and chewed determinedly through it.

In view of those batteries in the sacred divining rods, this was all extremely interesting. But why would the

High Priest be so keen on building a casino? If it'd been a café or a burger bar he could have understood it. And, as well, if the High Priest had got what he wanted, then why had he run away? With those batteries in the sacred divining rods, it meant that he could pass more or less any law he liked.

'What happens if the sacred divining rods throw out a law?' Sebastian asked Mr Walty next morning, over a plate of pastries.

Mr Walty sucked some icing slurpily off his thumb. 'Well, the High Priest or the apprentice opens the Sacred Texts at random, and they tell him what's wrong with the law.'

Sebastian took a bite at his pastry, to help him think.

'Yeah,' he said, indistinctly, 'but what if the law's about chewing gum, and the Sacred Text's all about snakes?'

'There aren't any snakes in the Sacred Texts,' said Mr Walty, irritably.

'No snakes?' echoed Sebastian, amazed.

'Of course not. Don't be silly. Well, let's suppose that the sacred divining rods have vetoed a law –'

'– about chewing gum.'

'Oh, very well. And then, let's suppose the Sacred Texts fall open at this passage here, which is the one we were going to study today in any case.'

'And then we can work out what the will of Ora would be,' said Sebastian.

'Humph,' said Mr Walty.

One day Ora was walking in the city and He came across a little boy with a glum face.

'Why is your face so long?' asked Ora.

'My tummy hurts,' replied the little boy.

'That is because it is full of green apples,' said Ora.

'I know,' said the little boy. 'Won't you make it better?' But Ora shook His head.

'I will not,' said Ora, 'because that is the way the world works, and the world is delightful to me, even though it is not perfect.'

'I wish it was perfect,' said the little boy, wistfully.

But Ora smiled, and said:

'If the world were perfect, then it would be part of me. And then I would be alone.'

'Oh,' said Sebastian, 'that's easy, then: it's saying that chewing gum's not even nearly perfect, isn't it?'

Mr Walty frowned.

'I suppose it is,' he agreed. 'Though we hardly needed Ora to tell us that. But it's also saying that the world, as it is, is delightful to Ora.'

'Oh,' said Sebastian, scratching his head. 'Yeah. But

then ... then it could mean anything, couldn't it?'

Mr Walty smiled rather grimly.

'Let's be very thankful that no apprentice has ever had the sacred divining rods reject any laws,' he said.

And the people of Ora prospered, and built a great city. And often, when they remembered how Ora had blessed them, they would bring Him a piece of honey-coloured stone as an offering of thanks and love.

And Ora kept all these stones and took great joy in the love of His people.

Chapter 15

Sebastian explained all about the new casino law to Gerald that evening.

'I expect the High Priest just wants to be helpful,' he said. 'I expect he *likes* being helpful. Anyway, a casino's a really good idea. I could just pop out whenever I was bored and have a nice game of cards or something. I mean, people *like* playing games, don't they? That's why the High Priest's made it so the sacred divining rods come up with the right answers all the time.'

Gerald looked up, sighed, and began cleaning his whiskers. He looked a bit tired, Sebastian thought: not as glossy as usual. Sebastian put down his hand for Gerald to climb onto, took him to their bedroom and put him down in his run. Gerald sat and panted for a little while, and then waddled towards his water bottle.

'You see,' said Sebastian, 'if you want to help people, you have to be able to do things, don't you? And Ora, well, He doesn't actually do anything very much any more.'

Gerald stopped drinking, blinked short-sightedly a couple of times, and waddled off towards his nest.

'Just think how much you could help people if you could get any laws passed you wanted,' said Sebastian.

'Just think what you could do.'

Sebastian watched Gerald burrow his way into his nest. And suddenly he had a feeling as if something inside him had turned a somersault.

He whispered the words again, carefully, so as not to disturb the Temple air.

'Just think,' he whispered. 'Just think what you could do.'

Later that evening there was an explosion in the marshes that lay to the west of the City. Birds flapped screaming and blundering into the twilight, and cats fled in swift and angry shadow. The massive gate house of the Golden Castle, traditional holiday residence of the High Priests of Ora, shivered, hung for a moment, and then crumbled into small pieces of rubble. In the Temple itself, the great golden lamp that shone perpetually above the Place of Offering wobbled, slopped oil, and began to swing.

The High Priest arrived at the Temple a couple of hours later, his watery blue eyes blinking out of a face flabby with bewilderment and black with soot. The cloak flung over his shoulders failed to hide the fact that the hems of his golden pyjamas were charred.

Turville and Sebastian stared at him, as if at an apparition.

'Gas main,' muttered the High Priest, one hand clutching protectively at his pyjama cord. 'Ker-boom.'

He lumbered hastily past them, and in a few moments several bolts were shot home on the inside of the door to his rooms.

Chapter 16

'Sorry I'm late,' said Mr Walty, irritably, the next morning. 'The headmaster kept me. Really, as if I can do anything about Horace Meeno's attendance record. I told the Head to contact the boy's guardians. That took the wind out of his sails, ha! Now, where were we? Oh yes.'

One day Ora was sitting by a fountain in the City when a woman came to him, weeping.

'Oh great god,' she said, 'bless Your holy name,' and she threw herself on the ground at His feet.

And Ora said, 'What troubles you?'

And the woman said:

'Truly, I have great trouble, for my husband, whom I love greatly, is sick and like to die. Oh, great Ora, who commands the world, fill him with your power and give him life.'

And Ora looked into the woman's mind and saw that she did indeed love her husband deeply. So He arose and went with the woman to the place where she lived and there He found the man, greatly sick, and in much pain.

And a great pity filled Ora, and He put out His power. But lo! As the power of the god filled the man, the breath fled from him; and he was no more.

And the woman let out a great cry, and said:

'I came to You in sorrow, and You have betrayed me!' And in her distress she went to strike Ora.

But Ora caught her hand, and embraced her, and He said: 'All that I make is perfect, and your kind cannot be so. So now your husband lives as part of me. And he was a good man.'

And they wept together.

Sebastian shifted uncomfortably in his seat.

'That wasn't much of a story,' he said.

Mr Walty sighed, but not impatiently.

'Certainly not a happy story,' he said.

'No,' said Sebastian. 'What should have happened, is that Ora should have flown through the air like a jet plane, and then made the bloke better.'

'Do you think so?' said Mr Walty.

'And then, they should have had a feast with pizza and ice-cream and jelly and cake and stuff. That would have been a lot happier. See?'

'Yes,' said Mr Walty. 'But the Sacred Texts aren't necessarily about providing happy endings.'

Sebastian frowned, thought about having another pot of chocolate mousse, and discovered he didn't want it.

'In all the stories ... Ora never *does* much,' said

Sebastian.

'No,' said Mr Walty. 'That's true, on the whole.'

'And just think of all the things *I've* done since I've been here: the train, and the parachute jump, and the bungee-jumping and all that. I mean, why don't you hear about Ora doing something really brilliant like a parachute jump?'

'Probably because the Sacred Texts were written before people invented aeroplanes.'

Sebastian sat and felt dissatisfied. It was a very rare thing for him to feel, and he didn't like it.

'And why doesn't Ora ever play football?' he asked, and suddenly realized he hadn't played football for ages. Not for weeks. And he found that there was a big uncomfortable thing inside him, like a balloon, which was going to get more and more uncomfortable until he played football. He even wondered if he might be going to *die* unless he played football.

'We never do sport,' he said suddenly. 'Why don't we do sport?'

Mr Walty's hand hovered over yet another pot of mousse. There were three well-scraped pots next to him already, and Sebastian had discovered that Mr Walty had an annoying habit of digging his spoon right down into the chocolate bit straight away, instead of scooping the cream off the top like everyone else.

‘Well,’ said Mr Walty, a bit shiftily, ‘you’ve always been busy doing other sporting activities, like your abseiling and snorkelling and croquet.’

‘Let’s play football, now, then,’ said Sebastian.

‘Oh, but ... I’m not really a qualified sports teacher,’ said Mr Walty, uneasily. ‘And in any case I’m really hardly dressed –’

‘That’s all right. Turville will find you something to wear,’ said Sebastian and rang the bell.

Mr Walty was the most annoying football player in the universe. He was even worse than Horace Meeno, who always played the ankle, not the ball, and who (it was said) sharpened his elbows before each game. Mr Walty was even worse than Robert, who never passed the ball until the only way he *could* pass the ball was for a corner. Mr Walty had absolutely no intention of running under any circumstances: he was the sort of person who, given a football, would put the other person in goal, blast penalties at them, and then expect a break to put his hands on his knees and gasp every time he put one in.

Chapter 17

The High Priest remained locked and bolted behind his door, but he seemed quite happy. He sang for hours on end; but when the next morning Councillor Kimber arrived, very shiny-faced and coldly determined, Turville had to report that the High Priest was unfortunately indisposed.

'His Omniscience was ever so shaken up by that simply awful explosion,' said Turville, regretfully. 'I think he had a little bit of something to calm his nerves and then he seems to have got a bit carried away.'

A glint, perhaps of satisfaction, appeared in Councillor Kimber's eyes.

'Well, then,' he said. 'In that case the apprentice can oblige.'

Councillor Kimber fanned out the papers and laid them on the desk. Sebastian ran his fingers exploringly along the rods. Yes, there were the pressure plates that turned on the bulbs. All he had to do was press just there, and –

And he could do anything he liked.

'Right, apprentice. If you'd just pass the rods over these papers here ... Excellent. And this next batch, here, if you please. All correct? Good. And now these ...

splendid, splendid. And just these very last ones, please, Your Knowingness and we'll be up straight.'

Changing a law would really get up Councillor Kimber's nose: why, he was still mad about the casino. But ... but it was no good. Sebastian just couldn't resist it. His fingers tightened on the pressure plates and the bulbs at the ends of the rods went from gold to bright glowing red.

'Got a bit of a problem,' said Sebastian. Councillor Kimber looked up. He stared at the bulbs on the ends of the rods and he went white and then red and then white again.

'But that's the new schools bill,' he said. 'There can't be any objection to that!'

'Why not?' said Sebastian. 'Just because it's to do with children, it doesn't mean that you can do anything you like to them without it being wrong.'

Councillor Kimber was suddenly so white that his blue eyes looked dark and almost dangerous.

'People do things to children that aren't even allowed with grown-ups,' Sebastian went on, warming to his theme. 'Like making them eat things they don't like. I mean, there isn't a law saying everyone has to eat sprouts, is there? Not for grown-ups. Is there? So it can't be important, can it? I mean, you don't see things on the television about hundreds of people dropping dead because of sprout deficiency, do you? I mean, do you? So that's probably what it is,' ended up Sebastian, triumphantly.

'*A sprout law?*' breathed Councillor Kimber and he hissed like a snake when he said it.

Turville drew in a deep breath.

'We'll have to consult the Sacred Texts,' he said. 'And may Ora bring down the light of His wisdom upon us.'

The volume Turville brought was just the ordinary everyday one that Sebastian used in lessons.

'Well, we haven't needed a special one,' said Turville, pointedly. 'Not until these last few weeks, at any rate.'

Sebastian let the book fall open. The ink had blotted on one sentence, making it stand out.

The wise shall drink from the fountain of knowledge all their lives long, it said.

'There,' said Turville, after Sebastian had read it out. 'That's a nice thought, isn't it? Just like His Knowingness was saying about the sprouts: we all know they're good for us, but we don't bother, a lot of the time, do we. Perhaps there should be a sprout-eating law. Do you think that's what it is, Your Knowingness?'

Sebastian paused to imagine all those grown-ups

shovelling down big plates of sprouts; of a great sprout festival, where people would sell hot sprouts from barrows in the street and the whole city would smell of sprouts.

Errrrgh.

And the thing was, that people's taste buds went funny as they got older, so that grown-ups actually quite often *liked* sprouts: which would be no fun at all.

'It's not about sprouts,' said Sebastian.

Councillor Kimber suddenly sat down.

'Look, this is terribly serious,' he said. 'This is no joke at all. The Council will never brook any more interference. It's undermining the whole system of government. This might well be the final straw.'

'What does the text mean, Your Knowingness?' asked Turville.

Sebastian thought. What could it mean? Something to do with schools. He could ban school uniform, or maths: except that Sebastian had a deep-down feeling that that would cause really so much trouble that even he might not get away with it.

And then he had an inspiration.

'It's to do with teachers,' he said. 'They've all got to do more training: *drink from the fountain of knowledge all their lives long*, get it?'

Councillor Kimber seemed to be having some trouble breathing.

'More training? And where's the budget going to come from for that?' he snapped.

'Oh, not that sort of training,' said Sebastian, hastily. 'No. They've all got to ... er ... do exercises.'

Councillor Kimber's eyes were bulging.

'Exercises?'

'Yes. Ball control,' said Sebastian, promptly. 'And ... er ... running. That sort of thing. Jumping up and down. To set a good example to the children.'

Sebastian had a sudden vision of Mr Walty and a wonderful idea came to him.

'And they have to go on commando courses,' he said. 'All the teachers from a school together. You know, through the jungle,' Sebastian went on, his heart beating fast with pleasure at the thought.

'Jungle?' yelped Councillor Kimber, as if someone had stuck a pin into him.

'The moors,' amended Sebastian, suddenly remembering that there wasn't a jungle within five hundred miles. 'And they have to survive and stuff,' he went on: 'Cook baked beans over a fire and build their own shelters.'

Councillor Kimber seemed to have been struck dumb: so Sebastian explained some more.

'It'll remind them what it's like being a child again,' he said. 'They'll be at the mercy of the elephants, just like children are at the mercy of their teachers.'

Councillor Kimber swallowed something brick-like and found part of his voice.

'Elephants?' he said, faintly.

'Yeah, you know, the wind and the rain and stuff. Do them good.'

Sebastian felt a surge of warmth spread through him at the rightness of it. Nice Mrs Burns would be all excited and cheerful and have a whale of a time and Mr Walty would get drips down the back of his neck. Perfect.

Councillor Kimber was suddenly looking almost wistful.

'I must say it would have done my chemistry teacher a lot of good,' he said. 'A terrible bully, he was.'

Sebastian sighed blissfully. There the headmaster and Mr Walty would be, crouched in a little tent over a pan of burnt beans, while the rain lashed down and bled the dye from the headmaster's gown.

Sebastian really felt that he'd made the world a better place.

But Councillor Kimber paused in the doorway.

'You know, this can't be allowed,' he said.

Sebastian was profoundly disappointed.

'You mean you can stop it?'

Councillor Kimber shook his head.

'No, I can't. But someone will. If this sort of thing goes on, then terrible things will happen and I won't be able to stop them, either. Do you understand, apprentice? Things will be out of control. And there needs to be control. Remember that.'

And he turned and shut the door firmly behind him.

Chapter 18

'These Sacred Texts,' said Sebastian. 'They're all about ordinary dull people. Why aren't the Sacred Texts about anyone interesting?'

'What do you mean, interesting?'

'People who do things, like ... like robbers and criminals. Exciting stories like that.'

Mr Walty flicked through the pages.

'How about this?' he said.

And it came to pass in the days of the first Council there was a man in the City who caused great grief to all his neighbours. He was a vicious man, who brawled and quarrelled, and all the City was quite honestly fed up to the back teeth with him.

'Sounds like Eunice,' said Sebastian.

And so the Council went to the Temple, and they stood before the place where the great statue of Ora would stand when they had managed to scrape together enough gold to make it, and they said:

'O great Ora, bless Your holy name!' And they told Ora all about the man. And the chief man of the Council said:

'This man is a bad man: he causes grief to everyone in the

City, and especially to the people who live in his street. It is in our minds to put him on a fast donkey, attach a firework to its tail, and point it at the mountains; although this would only be a majority decision, because some of us favour tying him to the mast of my third cousin's boat, which he never uses since he got his new one with the cabin and the deckchairs and everything, and letting it drift towards the great waterfall.'

And Ora appeared in a flash of lightning, in the place where His statue was going to be, and all the Council bowed low before His glory. And Ora said:

'That man is truly a bad man, but still do I love him, as I love all those who have been given life. And if you send him away from the City, a little part of me shall go with him, for I shall love him still.'

And then the head man of the Council said:

'Verily this is a knotty problem: it calls for much thought.'

And Ora smiled on them, and said, 'That is the purpose of the Council, grey-headed ones.'

And at that the Council took courage. And instead of banishing the man, they set him to work sticking pieces of paper on badly parked wagons. And this filled the man with so much joy that he had hardly any bad temper left to abuse his neighbours.

And so the City dwelt in peace.

* * *

Sebastian's was a busy life: on the day of the first sheep-jumping show Sebastian was so tied up all day he didn't get a chance to open his post until dinner time.

There were half a dozen letters with hearts drawn all over them: he got lots of them. They'd be wanting a signed photo–perhaps the nice one of him in a diving helmet from that time he did the river-bed walk. Apart from that, there was a loopy-lettered envelope from Mrs Blewitt and a small parcel.

It was all stuck down with duct tape and it said, PERSONAL AND CONFIDENTIAL.

'Hey, Turville,' said Sebastian, 'do you think you could open this for me? I'm all over peanut butter.'

'Of course, Your Knowingness. Ooh, it's from someone in the City. I wonder what it is, it's ever so heavy for its size. I'll just slit the –'

BOOOOOOOOOOOOOOM!

Sebastian sat still for some time and blinked through the smoke that was deflating all around him.

Then the smoke cleared a bit more and he saw that Turville was *black*: from his fair hair to his blue silk shirt to his corn-coloured socks he was as black as a mousehole at midnight.

Sebastian began to laugh, gasped in a mouthful of gritty smoke and choked, instead. Then a tiny cinder alighted on his hand and stung it and he realized that actually it might not be all that funny.

'Are you all right?' he asked.

Turville opened his eyes one at a time. They were so amazingly bright in his smut-covered face that they were almost glowing.

There was a pause.

'I think so, Your Knowingness,' he said, at last. 'Rather surprised.'

'Cor, yeah,' agreed Sebastian. 'And now the parcel's all spoiled. I wonder what was in it?'

Turville gazed down at the wisps of blackened wreckage that remained in his hands: a few bits of wire and some twists of metal.

'It's lucky you didn't burn your hands,' said Sebastian. 'I wonder what it was? Looks as if it might have been a clock or something. Must have got wet in the post. Dangerous, it can be, getting electricity and water mixed up.'

Turville took a deep breath. It was fascinating, because you could see the smoke going up his nose as he did it.

'Perhaps we'd better be a bit more careful about opening parcels in future,' he said, at last. 'Perhaps it might be an idea if I ordered some X-ray equipment.'

Sebastian was pleased.

'And then we'll be able to take pictures of each other's bones,' he said. 'I wonder what a rat skeleton looks like?'

Turville looked at Sebastian, opened his mouth, but then only sighed.

'You'd better go and have a shower and find a clean robe, Your Knowingness. And I'll see about getting things cleaned up. Ooh, and just look at me: I can see I'm going to have to take myself shopping this afternoon. There's a boutique down one of the streets by the market square that I've been meaning to try out for ages.'

'Cor, that was exciting, wasn't it? Pity about the parcel, though.'

And Sebastian went off to find Gerald, to tell him all about it.

A small figure slipped oozily into the Temple during Offerings that afternoon. It watched the High Priest's apprentice as he slid swiftly down the zip-wire to land with a drum-roll and a blinding flash of sodium flare right by the Place of Offering.

And it didn't look at all pleased.

Chapter 19

In the time of the eighth Council there was a High Priest whose name was Gurdlepod.

'Gurdlepod?' echoed Sebastian, choking on his popcorn. 'What kind of a name is Gurdlepod?'

'Well,' said Mr Walty, rather testily, for he had not been thrilled at the COMPULSORY GAMES FOR TEACHERS headlines that the newspapers had proclaimed that morning, 'for that matter, what sort of a name is Blewitt?'

'Well, at least blewits[1] are real,' pointed out Sebastian. 'At least they're tasty. Nothing like a blewit[1] omelette and chips, is there? Bet a Gurdlepod omelette would be revolting. Anyway, what's a gurdle?'

Mr Walty sighed from the depths of his being and read on.

Now, Gurdlepod was a man of weak mind, and what mind he had was consumed with his own importance. He made a decree that wherever he went all the people should bow down before him. And the people were obedient to him. But Gurdlepod grew so inflated with pride that he forgot his place as the servant of the people.

---

[1] a blewit is a type of mushroom

And it came to pass that he went into the Temple in the new hat that he'd caused to have made for the Wassail Feast, which was covered in golden pom-poms and had many ribbons under the chin.

But there was in that place a little child, a boy, who, when he saw the High Priest's hat, laughed so mightily that Gurdlepod was much angered; and Gurdlepod the High Priest seized the child, to beat him with his rod of office.

'The headmaster wears a funny hat,' said Sebastian, thoughtfully. 'Don't know why; it doesn't even keep his ears warm. But it's all flat on top, so I think it might be so that he can put things on it when his hands are full. You know, like sandwiches and stuff. Mind you, you'd have to be careful not to walk outside if it was sandwiches, because then I bet you'd get loads of seagulls swooping round and pinching stuff.'

'Don't be fatuous,' said Mr Walty, irritably and read on.

But Ora appeared in a flash of gold and stayed Gurdlepod's hand.

And then was Gurdlepod highly angry, and he spoke to Ora and he said: 'Unhand me! For I am the High Priest, and the most important part of the Wassail Feast.'

And Ora smiled, and said: 'So be it.'

And the sacred hat with the golden pom-poms and the great bunches of ribbons fell to the floor, and to the terror of the people it was seen that Ora and Gurdlepod had gone; and when at last the vergers gathered courage to pick up the hat, they found underneath it a fine turkey.

And since that day, turkey has been the most important part of the Wassail Feast, in memory of Gurdlepod. But Gurdlepod himself was not eaten, but sent to spend the rest of his life on a farm, where he made a much better turkey than he ever had a High Priest, and so lived happily ever after.

'That was a good story,' said Sebastian. 'I like turkey.'

'Hm,' said Mr Walty. 'And it shows how dangerous it would be to get on the wrong side of Ora, bless His holy name, doesn't it? It'd be very foolish, for instance, to do anything to alter His will as regards the laws of the City.'

'Oh,' said Sebastian. 'Yeah, course. Still, that's all right, that was all ages ago. Ora doesn't really do much nowadays, does He? And, besides, I never was much of a one for hats.'

Chapter 20

The phone went next morning while Sebastian was giving Gerald a ride in the table-top train. Gerald hadn't liked the train, much, until Sebastian had started putting chocolate drops into his carriage, but now he seemed to look forward to his ride.

'Temple of Ora.'

'Sebastian, darling? I'm afraid something absolutely terrible has happened, dear.'

Sebastian felt a flicker of interest. Perhaps Robert had broken a leg.

'What?'

'I'm terribly sorry, but they've changed the date of the Debating Society final.'

'So what?' asked Sebastian, keeping a sharp eye out to make sure that Gerald didn't get his tail caught up on anything.

'I'm afraid it's been changed to this evening, darling.'

It took a moment for the full horror of the situation to hit him.

'You don't mean I've got to listen to some boring debating stuff!'

'I'm terribly sorry,' said Mrs Blewitt, 'but–'

'Listening to Eunice spouting on,' Sebastian went on,

bitterly. 'Rabbiting on for hours and hours on end and all about nothing. And all the others as well. Drives you mad. And on my evening off!'

'Oh dear, darling. The thing is, I promised I'd go and hear Eunice, or else of course I'd –'

'I mean, I work the rest of the week,' said Sebastian, hugely aggrieved. 'Work my fingers to the bone receiving offerings and stuff. All I get is two evenings a week to come home. Just two evenings in the whole week–and then I have to go and listen to Eunice drivelling on. It'd be better to stay here!'

There was a short pause and then Mrs Blewitt said, almost hopefully:

'Would you rather stay at the Temple, darling? It'd only be for tonight, wouldn't it and then we could do something really special next time you come. We could read some poems together. How about that?'

Sebastian stopped the train and let Gerald climb out onto his sleeve. *Stay at the Temple? Well, why not.* Gerald was all the company anyone could want. Turville always went out for the night on a Tuesday, but Sebastian would be fine by himself.

'All right,' he agreed, with a brave show of reluctance and regret. 'I expect I'll manage. Yes, yes, I'll be all right. Yes. Goodbye.'

* * *

Mr Walty arrived a little late, extremely put-out.

'It's this dreadful teacher-training-for-life football team,' he said, darkly. 'The headmaster seems to think he should be captain. *Ha!* A man who still thinks the shoulder barge is legal. And he kept complaining when his goal was disallowed, even though everyone saw it went a clear yard outside the near-side jumper. Still,' he went on, brightening a little, 'we're going to have proper goalposts with nets next week.'

Sebastian called up a vision of the headmaster out of breath and covered in mud and felt pleased.

'What about the lady teachers?' he asked. 'Are they playing football too?'

'Oh no, no, not as a rule. They can if they like, of course, but they're organizing their own activities: synchronized rambling and peace-contortion and power-knitting. That sort of thing. They seem quite keen. Now, where were we?'

One day Ora was walking in the City when he saw some children playing merrily; but when He approached them He saw that there, in a box, was a cat with a bell tied to its tail, which made it spit and fight in terror.

And a shade fell over the heart of Ora, and He said: 'What is there in this ugly thing that makes you laugh and play?' And the children put their heads on their chests and they were silent.

And Ora was angry, and He felt no love in Himself for them, and He said: 'Be good!'

Sebastian shifted in his chair.

'But Ora doesn't do things like that any more, does He?' he said, a little anxious.

Mr Walty sighed.

'Not any more,' he said. 'But just imagine what it would be like if He did! Polite, respectful, hardworking children ... Happy, tranquil teachers ...'

'So what happened?'

'This happened,' said Mr Walty, gloomily.

And behold, a great peace fell over the City.

And on the first day it came to pass that all the grown-ups had such an easy time that they didn't know what to do with themselves; and on the second day they all went to the dump to get rid of all the rubbish the children had found when they'd tidied their rooms; but on the third day, a great crowd of the people went to Ora and said: 'Great god, holy and blessed is Your name, and mighty is Your wisdom, but can we have our children back, please? We know they are noisy and rude and thoughtless, but the sight of them getting up early to do good deeds is giving us the willies; and, besides, they are beginning to annoy the old folk who do not wish to keep crossing the road.'

And Ora was moved, and He lifted His command from the children, and He said: 'Verily, you are none of you even nearly perfect: but you have shown Me a more perfect love.'

And the people were content.

Sebastian didn't mention anything to Turville about staying at the Temple. Turville always looked forward to his evening off and would certainly feel obliged to stay behind if he knew Sebastian was going to be there.

'A night away at the Priest's Head, I think,' he said. 'I always enjoy the Priest's Head, as long as the karaoke machine's broken. Which I must say it always is. And someone to make my breakfast in the morning. Have you finished with the food on the table?'

'Yeah,' said Sebastian, picking up a last cold, sludgy profiterole. 'Thanks.'

Turville loaded up a tray and then got to work with the table brush.

'Thanks,' said Sebastian, again.

'It's not easy, cleaning up round a train set,' said Turville.

Sebastian ordered the limo while Turville was hair-spraying his eyebrows and then had Bert drive him round and round the City while he treated himself to a nice bottle of lemonade from the fridge.

The limo, being gold and flaggy, always attracted lots of attention, but Sebastian enjoyed the waving. He'd had Turville organize him a special waving stick. It had gold and red stripes, with a big inflatable hand on the end and Sebastian found it cheered up everyone a treat: even the dogged old ladies with shopping trolleys couldn't help giggling to themselves as he sailed past. The only person who didn't smile was Finley Wortle, who was pacing up and down under the cream-honey portico of the Temple bearing his lonely placard, which today read:

HAPPINESS IS FREE – AND SO SHOULD WE BE

Sebastian spoke into the tube and Bert slid the limo to a halt just at the end of Finley's beat. Finley's trousers were sagging under his armpits, as usual, and he was wearing his usual moth-eaten tie, even though, this evening, the sun was shining down and turning the whole City to a miracle of voluptuous honeycomb and fretwork shadows.

'Fancy a doughnut?' asked Sebastian. 'I've got chocolate, vanilla, or peanut butter.'

Finley, about to turn away, hesitated.

'Peanut butter?' he enquired, gruffly.

'Yeah,' said Sebastian. 'You can have two if you want.'

A wistfulness came across Finley's face, but then he resettled his grip firmly on the handle of his placard and drew himself to attention.

'Parasites!' he said, very business-like. 'Liars! Traders in brain-soap!'

'Yeah,' said Sebastian, patiently. 'But the peanut butter doughnuts are all right. Would you like one?'

Finley opened his mouth, but he seemed to be involved in some huge struggle, because no sound came out.

'I'll tell you what,' said Sebastian. 'I'll get Bert to leave a couple on the stone turkey's head, all right? See you later, then. Bye!'

Chapter 21

When Sebastian let himself back into his rooms, all that was left of Turville's presence was a neatly-hung tea towel and some items on the memo board in nice handwriting.

Sebastian had a satisfactory supper of bread and dripping and then amused himself by laying a chocolate drop trail for Gerald. Gerald was a long way outside his personal best for the route, according to Sebastian's new stopwatch, but then Gerald did stop twice to clean his whiskers. Gerald was probably a bit bored with doing the same old course all the time.

Sebastian wondered about working out something more interesting, with doors to open and stuff. There was no point in having a really intelligent rat like Gerald if you just got him to –

A dark shape slid past the window.

That was funny. Everyone was supposed to be out, except for the High Priest and he was barricaded behind a triple-bolted door that couldn't be opened even with the aid of the extremely powerful magnet that Turville had obtained from the University Physics department.

There was a jingling and then a key was fitted into the lock on the outside door.

Turville, already? Bringing some friends home? Or

someone else? Sebastian gently scooped up Gerald and retreated into the larder. It was a large walk-in affair, not even half full since Sebastian had got Turville to buy the coffin-freezer so they could make four-foot long raspberry lollies where you had to hold the stick with your feet. Sebastian closed the door gently. The larder was by far the best place in the Temple to get stuck if you were going to have to be stuck somewhere. Sebastian let Gerald waddle off quietly onto the biscuit shelf and he listened.

There seemed to be quite a lot of people coming through the back door and into the lobby. Turville? Bert? Mrs Poash?

Then there was a voice:

'Throw the bolt on the door, Jerome.'

That wasn't anyone from the City. That was a harsher voice, with an outsider's accent.

'Sure, boss.'

Sebastian put his eye to the keyhole, but all he could see was a bit of chair leg and some tablecloth.

'Hey, boss!'

A different voice.

'What is it, Harry?'

'There's a light showing under the door.'

Pause.

'Check it out, Harry.'

Sebastian heard the door into the kitchen open and for some reason he found himself holding his breath.

'Just dirty plates and some crumbs, boss.'

'Hm. Don't like that, Harry. Don't like that at all.'

'Probably just left out by some guy, boss.'

'Well, that's what you think, Harry, and that's why I'm the boss, see? Just ask yourself how it was I got to the top of this here organization.'

'Because you hit Duane the Chain and Char the Scar, boss.'

'Yeah, I'm ruthless, sure. But that housekeeper guy– the one that does the cooking and looks after the kid and the reverend – he's never one to leave things in a state of disarray. Do you get me?'

'Er ... sure, if you say so, boss.'

'That guy ain't never got so much as a hair out of place, let alone a whole set of plates complete with crumbs.'

'Perhaps it was the kid, boss.'

'Yeah. Maybe so. But I don't like it, Harry. You keep your optics wide open, OK?'

'Sure, boss.'

'So come on!'

The door closed and Sebastian very gently let out his breath. He peered through the keyhole again and then he opened the door just the tiniest crack.

Nothing.

He was pretty sure that Harry had gone through into the corridor with Mr Meeno, but where was Jerome? Jerome, the one (he remembered, now) who looked like a moth-eaten ape?

Not by the range, not by the window, not by the door ...

Nowhere. The room was quite empty. Gone into the corridor, then, with the others.

But what for?

Sebastian left Gerald safely on the biscuit shelf and slid out into the room.

Chapter 22

Sebastian had rehearsed this many times: Sebastian Blewitt, spy extraordinaire, on the track of –

Well, he wasn't quite sure what he was on the track of. Not yet, he wasn't.

The three men were making their way along the corridor. Two slant-cones of light bobbed along before them, sometimes pausing for a half-second on a door handle or zipping across a wall. Just occasionally there would be a shadow from something held close in a hand.

Sebastian narrowed his eyes thoughtfully and very nearly walked into the umbrella stand.

Sebastian hastily un-narrowed his eyes. This was real. Real gangsters, real secrets, real danger. Sebastian extricated a walking stick with extreme care from the stand and went on after the three black pieces of darkness that bobbed along in front of the reflected glow of the torches.

There wasn't much cover and Harry was as jumpy as a cat in a kennel. He turned right round, once, flashing his torch and Sebastian could only turn his head away and freeze, and hope.

The beam flicked across his robe and away. Sebastian went down on his hands and knees and crawled as fast as he could behind a knobbly cabinet.

Ahead were glimpses of corrugated foreheads and gleams of slicked-back hair.

Sebastian's heart leapt with fear and pleasure. This was even better than sending Mr Walty on survival courses.

'Boss!'

'What's up, Harry?'

'Thought I saw something move, boss.'

'Probably just the flashlight playing tricks. Hear anything?'

'Nah. All quiet.'

'Yeah. Too quiet, if you ask me. This place gives me the creeps.'

They were turning right. Sebastian waited until they were through the heavy door that shut off the High Priest's rooms from his own and then slipped over the tiled floor, holding his walking stick across him so it wouldn't trip him up.

Ahead came three heavy thumps and then the sound of splintering wood.

He followed the three figures, anyway.

Chapter 23

Along the faintly musty corridor a light shone through a door Sebastian had not seen open for some time. He went three careful steps further. Through the doorway a bleary figure in a nightcap was sitting, open-mouthed and quivering, in a jumbled bed.

'Mr Meeno,' it was saying, 'Oh great Ora, great Ora, great Ora preserve me. I thought the door was bolted. I'm sure –'

The shortest of the silhouettes between Sebastian and the doorway shrugged expansively.

'Sure, HP. But I don't generally do house calls, so as I'd taken the trouble to come, Jerome here just applied a little pressure with his shoulder. Applying force is one of his talents, see? Though I am being more than somewhat generous, because Jerome does not in truth have many others, aside from crushing a human skull with one blow of his fist. Still, I like to keep him around, in case of dispute. Jerome!'

'Yes, boss?'

'Get me a drink. On the rocks.'

Jerome prowled massively out of sight and there came a noise like glass shivering.

Mr Meeno's silhouette strolled in the other direction,

and then there was a creaking of leather, as if of someone settling himself into an armchair.

'Hey, all you lot, sit down, sit down. Let's make this all nice and neighbourly, OK? That's right. That's more like it. I like to have things friendly, HP.'

'Oh. Good,' said the High Priest, with a gulp.

'Yeah. You see, HP, I like to think of my business associates as family. That's people like you, HP.'

'Erggh,' said the High Priest, into the long pause. 'That's ... er ... that's very nice.'

'Yeah. Sure is. It doesn't always do me any good, you understand, but I guess my heart's so soft I just can't help it. Like, say, imagine some poor guy has walked all the way up this hill. So what then? Well, I figure he wants a drink and maybe a nice relaxing game of blackjack. You see, HP, I'm what is known in educated circles as a philanthropist. It means I'm all heart. Ain't that so, Harry?'

'Sure, boss.'

'Ain't that so, Jerome?'

'Sure, boss.'

'Yeah. That's so. I have this strong desire to do good to my fellow men. Get me? And so, even when one of my business associates does a wrong thing – let's say he makes a mistake – then my natural affection makes it awkward for me to take what you might call disciplinary action.'

'Guk!' said the High Priest.

'Let's take a case in point,' carried on Mr Meeno, pleasantly. 'I find that my wishes regarding the apprentice have been ignored. Now, that's a shame. My heart is filled with little pictures of all the great kindnesses I could do to my fellow men if only I could be sure of co-operation in the divining rod department. Hey, HP?'

'But –'

'Don't talk across the boss,' growled Harry.

The High Priest made a sort of whooping gasp and clamped his mouth tightly shut.

'– now I guess you have some reasonable explanation,' went on Mr Meeno, smoothly, 'and I trust you are more than ready to make amends, but even so this delay to my plans is set to cost me a considerable heap of sugar. And when you have a big family, like me, then sweetness is kind of important, do you get me?'

The High Priest rocked and nodded his flabby chins earnestly and even managed to haul up an affirmative squeak.

'Now, a guy could be exceedingly put-out at being let down like that,' said Mr Meeno. 'When he has been impeded and delayed in that manner. He might even try to close down someone like that altogether.'

'Shall I hit him, boss?' asked Jerome, hopefully.

There was a pause. Sebastian reluctantly decided that if Mr Meeno gave the order to attack, then he would have to intervene. He'd switch the lights off, hit as many people over the head as he could with his walking stick and then scarper and hope the High Priest had the sense to do the same.

'Well ...' said Mr Meeno, reflectively, 'I guess the guy has broken his word. And it is not possible to do business with a guy whose word cannot be relied upon. I consider that a sign of a very wicked and immoral character, Jerome.'

'Shall I take off his ear, boss?'

Another long pause, filled only with a tiny whimpering.

'I don't know if we should do that,' said Mr Meeno, at last. 'It would relieve my feelings, sure ... but then, the HP is practically a sacred personage. And, besides, what if the HP was to turn up in the Temple with an ear missing? That would be naturally most distasteful to the citizens of this place.'

'Please,' came the High Priest's voice, shrill with terror. 'I'll do anything you say! You just tell me what to do and I'll do it. I'll do anything, anything!'

'It's not that easy, HP. We cannot afford to overload the system, there and your apprentice has been passing some laws of his own. That is another disappointment,' went on Mr Meeno, rather less smoothly. 'I went to the considerable trouble of pointing out to you the most suitable candidate for that job.'

'Yes! Yes, but –'

'A good boy, my nephew Horace: the right age, keen, does as he's asked. I like that in a boy. In fact, I like that in the general populace, HP. I feel it makes the world a happier place.'

'But I tried,' the High Priest was almost sobbing, now. 'Ora knows I tried. I did everything you said, didn't I? I let you have the sacred divining rods; I even put new batteries in them, just in case, before I left the Temple.'

'So what went wrong, HP? Cos the smart alec in the dress sure as bullets ain't my nephew Horace.'

'I don't know! I don't know. When I got to the classroom I was all prepared to point the divining rods at the young man and turn on the lights–but they just wouldn't go. They were too powerful for me. I did my best – *but they were dragging me across the classroom*!'

Someone yawned.

'I swear it's true! There was so much power there – there was nothing I could do against it. Oh great Ora, great Ora, what have I done to deserve this?'

There was a long pause while the High Priest moaned and hugged himself and blinked his watery eyes.

'Well,' said Mr Meeno, at last, 'I guess this City is a strange place. And, being a reasonable guy, I can see this Ora sort of goes with your job. I can see that. An organization has to have authority–and it has to have an executive force. Now, my executive force is invested in my friends here. And a man with friends like these guys ... well, let's just say that they are a great advantage to me because their loyalty fills up the place that would normally be occupied by their hearts. And me? Well, I guess I make up for them because I guess I'm just about all heart. It's true I've been held up a few days, but, hey, a big-hearted guy like me can get over that.'

'That's ... that's very kind of you, Mr Meeno,' said the High Priest.

'Yeah. Though it sure is strange the way things have gone. You know, if I wasn't a sweet trusting guy I might think you were trying to swing a double-cross.'

'Oh but –'

'So you said. And I sure hope that ain't the case, HP, because unfortunate things happen to people who try to double-cross me. Hey, Harry, do you remember that guy – what was his name – the one to whom we very kindly offered employment, and then it turned out that he was feathering his own nest?'

'Don't quite recall him, boss.'

'No? Well, he wasn't around for very long. I guess the guilt and remorse kind of got to him, because he was found in the river not long after that. He'd buried his feet in a carton of concrete and then jumped all the way up to the middle of the pilgrim's bridge and just thrown himself off. Tragic.'

'I'll ... I'll do my best for you,' whispered the High Priest.

'Sure you will. Just make sure it's good enough, huh? I guess we'll have to wait a little time for the next batch of laws to come along, but then I shall be requiring a small favour.'

'I'll do anything you say. Anything. Don't you worry. You can trust me, Mr Meeno.'

'I sure hope so, HP. Because my casino, it has run into a little difficulty on account of all the old buildings that clutter up your so-called Holy Hill. So I would appreciate it if the Council Chamber is pulled down, OK?'

The High Priest jolted as if someone had applied electrodes.

'The ... the –'

'Only the old one,' said Mr Meeno, reasonably. 'Just one old building without any use or purpose.'

The High Priest seemed to be finding it hard to breathe. He went slowly purple, then bone-white.

'OK?' snarled Harry's voice: and the High Priest's head sagged in submission and agreement.

Leather creaked again and Sebastian didn't wait. He slipped along the corridor and went and hid under his bath. He lay flat on his stomach as quick footsteps tacked along the corridor and someone fell with a clatter over the umbrella stand.

Sebastian gave them a considerable amount of time to leave the building. Then he made his way very cautiously and slowly back to the kitchen to pick up Gerald.

Sebastian set his alarm for half past five. He needed time to put everything back as it should be before the limo came to pick him up. He'd arranged for Bert to drive him round the City for a while so that Sebastian could stage a nice returning-from-a-night-at-home scene for Turville.

There was plenty of time to get everything straightened out before Turville got back. Sebastian even had time to check out the Temple.

The golden statue of Ora was gleaming in the first exploring rays of the dawn. Sebastian hesitated in front of it. He wondered what it was about being with the statue in the mornings that so often made

Mrs Poash cry.

Ora never did anything, nowadays. He'd even let Mr Meeno take over things in the City.

But perhaps ... perhaps He'd chosen Sebastian as apprentice.

Sebastian shrugged and plunged back to his quarters to look out for the limo.

Chapter 24

Being a gangster was all that Sebastian had ever wanted to be and there was no doubt that putting batteries in the sacred divining rods so that you could make your own laws was quite brilliant, but somehow Sebastian found it hard to shake off the image of the High Priest's face, wobbling with terror.

It may have been all the excitement, but Sebastian found himself feeling a bit sluggish, just like Gerald seemed to be. He even abandoned his new Offerings routine that involved roller blades, party poppers and a whole swarm of clockwork bees and whenever the Offerings bell went he just said, 'Ta, nice to meet you,' grabbed whatever it was and headed back to his quarters to have a sit down.

Turville hesitated after he'd served up Sebastian's evening meal.

'Some of the offerers have been talking,' he said.

'Oh?'

'Yes. They said you haven't been your usual self the last day or two. No rope swinging. No belly-dancing. Not even any dry ice, or the musical whoopee cushions.'

'Yeah, so?'

Turville paused.

'Well, they were disappointed, Your Knowingness. You've become quite an attraction. You're a character, that's what you are: an original. Someone who doesn't go by the usual rules.'

Like Mr Meeno, thought Sebastian and wasn't sure if he was pleased.

'Even the vergers are worried,' went on Turville.

'But I thought the vergers didn't like all the new stuff,' said Sebastian; their noses had been getting higher and their mouths lower with each new routine.

'Oh, don't worry about that,' said Turville. 'They love being disgusted, it's what they come for. If it wasn't you, it'd be the make of floor polish or the height of someone's heels. No, Your Knowingness, you keep them busy and they love it. And I'm sure I've often seen a bit of foot-tapping when the band gets going. And I saw one of them smile, the other day.'

'You didn't!'

'Yes I did.'

'What, had someone broken his ankle or something?'

'Don't be wicked. No. Actually, I think it was a sign of happiness.'

* * *

'Are all the laws of the City made up by the Council?' asked Sebastian, when Mr Walty came.

Mr Walty frowned.

'Until just recently, yes,' he said, rather sourly. 'Until the recent extremely dubious incidents.'

Sebastian scowled in thought.

'So – things like not stealing, or killing people, or making offerings. That's all made up by the Council.'

Mr Walty ran a hand through his hair.

'Well, no,' he admitted.

'But you just said –'

'If you'll listen, Blewitt, you might find out.'

One day Ora was walking in the City. The sun made all the City glow gold, and He was very happy. But wherever He went He heard voices raised in anger, and He could find no peace. So He went to the High Priest, and He said, 'It is my wish that you make a law that the people shall live in peace and happiness and not argue about whose turn it is to empty the chamber-pot, or whose fault it was that syllabub got spilled all down that jerkin that'd only been washed last month, or who left that ploughshare just where people were going to fall over it.'

And the High Priest, who was called Kurdle, and was wise, said: 'Oh great Ora, the people love and respect You, and listen to Your words; but such things are very difficult for them. And, besides, laws are things that vanish on the wind, for they are not set in stone.'

And Ora said, 'They are now'; and a great boulder

appeared from the sky and fell to earth, and on it were inscribed the sacred words of Ora's wishes for His people.

And Kurdle had to shout at the top of his voice for several hours before he could get out, for the stone blocked the door.

'Cor!' said Sebastian. 'Did it bring the roof down?'

Mr Walty scratched his head.

'Well ... it doesn't say,' he said.

'I bet it did. I bet it came down just like a bomb and there were tiles and rafters flying all over the place. Mr Walty!'

'Well?'

'I was wondering if we could train an elephant to come down on a platform from the dome.'

Mr Walty sat opening and closing his mouth for some time. And then he sighed.

'I think it would be difficult to train an elephant to stand on a platform, Blewitt,' he said. 'And just think what an elephant might do if it got out of control.'

Sebastian's eyes lit up.

'Cor, yeah! That'd be brilliant, wouldn't it? All the vergers and great-aunts running about and screaming – and the bookstalls going flying –'

'And people getting hurt and the Temple being disfigured by gold-leafed tusks,' said Mr Walty, drily.

Sebastian stopped and thought and sighed.

'Yeah. Suppose so. I mean, it was quite dangerous when all those people got gas-poisoning after we got that cow in. The ambulance people said it was lucky I was wearing my oxygen mask, ready to do my mountaineering routine, or it might have killed me. They said it was the first case they'd known of a cow's wind being so poisonous. Still, it was a good idea, wasn't it? People would have loved it. It would have brought in hundreds of people to the Temple, I bet: thousands, even.'

'It was certainly a remarkable idea. Yes, I have to agree with you there, Blewitt.'

'Yeah,' said Sebastian. 'And I've got *loads* more where that came from.'

At the end of Offerings the next day (Sebastian, encouraged, had reinstated the pogo-stick yodellers and the twinkling smoke rings) he made his way down the aisle between its delicate chair-end lattices of golden flowers and bees and into the shadow of the porch. The offerers nodded and smiled and while none of the stiff-haired vergers went that far, none of them actually spat, or held their noses as he went past. Even Mrs Poash only looked at him as if he were a spider in a teacup.

So things could have been worse.

The sun was just beginning to slip peacefully into evening when Sebastian stepped out through the great heavy door onto the golden flagstones of the portico.

There was still plenty of traffic down on the main road by the river, but up here there was hardly a vehicle to disturb the evening calm. He stood and breathed the air.

And then a shadow fell on him. It was cast by a sandwich board which proclaimed:

FREEDOM FROM TYRANNY
DOWN WITH THE TEMPLE

'Oh, hi,' said Sebastian. 'All right?'

Finley sighed deeply and shifted the leather bands that hung over his round shoulders.

'Cor, but it's been a hot one, today. Be glad to get home and put my feet up, I will.'

Finley's heavy boots were dusty and he smelt sourly of sweat: his combed-across hair was stuck down with it.

'You can always come in for a drink or a sit down, any time,' said Sebastian. 'Turville would be happy to find you something.'

For a moment Finley's sad face lightened: but then it fell back into its usual discouraged grooves and he shook his head.

'Nah,' he said. 'Not from you lot.'

'But why not?' said Sebastian. 'You could come round the back. No one would know.'

But Finley shook his head still more decisively, so that the clip holding his hair across his bald scalp wagged forlornly.

'Nah,' he said again. 'It's very nice of you, young man and don't think I don't appreciate it, but I'm not lapping crumbs from the table of the priests and vergers.'

'You could sit on the doorstep, then,' said Sebastian. 'Turville does a lovely Knickerbocker Glory with extra everything. He even tops it off with a golden dome made of sugar.'

And Finley sighed, but still shook his head.

'It's a matter of conscience,' he said, with regret. 'Oh, I don't blame you, because you're too young to know what's going on, but, you see, it's not right. It makes no sense at all, lad.'

'People seem happy enough,' pointed out Sebastian.

'Ah, but they're not. I mean, you can't look at those vergers of yours and say they're happy, can you? Giving up their lives because they're afraid what Ora will do to them, that's what they're doing. Tragic.'

'But Ora doesn't do things to people,' said Sebastian. 'Not any more.'

Finley shook his head sadly.

'And that's the pity of it. Something terrible happens and what do they do? Realize there's no such thing as God, or Ora, or whatever you want to call Him? Get on with their lives? No, they run back to the Temple like whipped puppies. Terrible! Terrible!'

'But that's what they want,' said Sebastian.

Finley sighed.

'Perhaps it is,' he admitted. 'You know, I've walked up and down this portico, day in, day out, for thirty-three years. I've told everyone who's walked through that door that they're wasting their time; that there's no point in throwing good money at a golden statue. I mean, it's just plain good sense! But sometimes I wonder if I've really made a difference.'

'Oh, but you're famous,' said Sebastian. 'Everyone knows you. You're even in the Tourist Guide. And that day you went to the dentist, the vergers were complaining like mad because that's all people asked them about, where you were. Wanted to know where they put their offerings for Finley, they did.'

Finley's face lifted into a bashful smile.

'Did they really? Well, I do get the odd donation to help the cause of atheism. Keeps me in boots and bread, that does. And I get my grant from the Arts Council, of course. People can be very kind. Even Mr Meeno has offered to help with my photocopying. And sometimes I think that now that the laws of the City are being changed, people are beginning to sit up and take notice, at last. You'd be surprised how long it is since I've had a rotten tomato thrown at me: and you can't argue with a sign of popularity like that.'

Sebastian drew a football pitch in the dust with his

toe and placed his right foot on the penalty spot.

'It'd be all right if they were good laws that were made up,' he said. 'Then everything would be all right, wouldn't it?'

'Oh, you're a good lad. And you never know, maybe some day you'll all see sense about all this.'

He waved a stubby hand to indicate the Temple, standing in razor-edged glory in the sinking light. Sebastian watched Finley trundle away, his sandwich board restricting him to a rolling waddle and then Sebastian turned to go back into the peace of the Temple.

He had taken two steps when there was a movement in the air behind him and then a sound like several train crashes. Sebastian performed a movement usually only seen in ice-skating competitions, turned a hundred and eighty degrees and landed amongst a thousand spitting fragments of sandy stone.

One of the big stone hives that stood along the top of the portico had fallen, Sebastian realized, when his heart had fainted back into place and his eardrums had stopped buzzing like over-excited hornets. A gust of wind must have toppled it.

Sebastian looked out over the City at the setting sun. There was the faintest waft of air coming up from the river as it relaxed from its baking hotness, but you wouldn't have thought it was nearly enough to dislodge a big thing like that.

'Cor!' said Sebastian, gently and he wandered back into the Temple in search of restorative ice-cream.

A slick of black hair appeared over the edge of the portico roof, together with some clutching white knuckles. It was followed by a cheesy face, a snub nose and a curdling scowl.

It whispered something, too.

Chapter 25

There was a lot of fuss about the destruction of the Old Council Chamber to make room for the casino. Sebastian, like Mr Meeno, couldn't really see the problem.

'Well, it's the *Old* Council Chamber, isn't it?' he said. 'We've got a new one, now, haven't we?'

Apparently the Old Council Chamber was very nearly a thousand years old and was in fact almost the only thing on the Holy Hill that had escaped the Great Combustion.

'Yeah,' said Sebastian. 'But you don't keep things just because they're old, do you? You don't say, "Oh, this is my oldest jumper, so I'll keep it," and then throw away a newer one, do you? Do you, huh?'

Sebastian enjoyed watching the demolition. There was a bit of a scare when the chain holding back the big demolition ball snapped just when Sebastian was inspecting it: Sebastian would have been splattered all over the place if the chain hadn't got snagged on a girder, swung round massively and neatly destroyed the site-manager's office, instead.

The dust from the destruction covered the Holy Hill and filled the Temple with billions of lazily twirling motes of gold, so that even Mrs Poash looked moth-eaten by the end of her shift. Councillor Kimber was livid: he went about the City in a fuzz of resentment. And the lenses of his glasses shone red with glints of fiery rage.

Chapter 26

Turville came into Sebastian's rooms the next morning during lessons.

One day Ora was walking in the world, and He came across a young man with a long face.

'Why is your face so long?' asked Ora.

'Because I have been ploughing all day with an ox so foul tempered it makes my wife's mother seem sweet as honey,' he said. 'And when I get home, my house, which is much too small, will be shaking with the feet of my children, who are the noisiest in all the world and think I am a trampoline.'

And Ora waved His arm, and lo! The man's field was ploughed, deep and true; and at the end of the field was a house, and it was perfect, even down to the built-in clockwork spit in the kitchen.

And the man fell down on his face and gave thanks; but still his face was glum.

'But do you not like the shutters carved in precious woods, and the toning textured plaster in the hall?' asked Ora.

'They are perfect,' said the man, 'and great is your bounty; but I find that I wish that I could have done it myself.'

'But then you would have had to spend many more years of your life striving with your bad-tempered ox and

mother-in-law,' said Ora.

'Yes,' said the man, 'but I have arms and legs, and probably, on a good day, the patience, to do it. It seems right that I should use the gifts that I have been given.'

'But then your house and land would not have been perfect,' said Ora.

'No, great God,' said the man. 'But then they would have been truly mine.'

And then Ora understood that the people wished to make their own place, just as He had brought into being everything that exists.

And so He did not often walk openly in the world any more, though the people were constantly in His heart.

And the people prospered so that soon their minds were cluttered with business, and they did not often have time for Ora. But in their hearts they remembered Him, and honoured Him, and knew that He was there.

Turville sighed.

'That's one of my favourite stories,' he said. 'It's so sad, isn't it, but so lovely.'

Sebastian considered.

'I liked the bit about the clockwork spit,' he said. 'I never knew there was anything like that: is it sort of like a catapult, to make it go further?'

Mr Walty closed his eyes as if in pain.

‘Oh good grief,’ he murmured. ‘Turville, say something sensible, for Ora’s sake, before my brain becomes permanently warped.’

‘Well, I’m sorry to interrupt,’ said Turville, ‘but Councillor Kimber’s here with some more laws. And the thing is, I’m afraid His Omniscience is fast asleep. I think it must be delayed shock from the explosion: I mean, I’m still all of a flutter myself. Such a surprise, the gas main exploding, especially as, to my knowledge, they didn’t have gas laid on.’

‘I bet it was all that singing,’ said Sebastian. ‘He was still at it at four o’clock – I woke up and he was singing his heart out, he was.’

‘Oh,’ said Mr Walty. ‘I see.’

‘Practising for the autumn festival, I think,’ went on Sebastian. ‘Because it was all about melons and cherries. Good tune, too, I thought, but a bit sad, so I thought that perhaps I’d get the band to put a track down underneath it: you know, liven it up a bit.’

‘Er ... not that song, I don’t think,’ said Mr Walty, hurriedly.

Turville looked from one to the other.

‘Well, I don’t think I’m going to be able to wake His Omniscience up,’ he said. ‘He’s out as flat as a flounder. It’ll have to be His Knowingness, again, I’m afraid.’

Councillor Kimber was fanning out wads of paper

with capable hands.

'The Council doesn't half make a lot of laws,' said Sebastian, taking the divining rods off the cushion that Turville presented to him.

Councillor Kimber gave him a dark look through his white eyelashes.

'The City is a very complicated thing,' he said. 'And keeping things fair and safe for everybody isn't an easy matter.'

'Oh,' said Sebastian. 'Right.'

He passed the divining rods across the first fan of paper. Councillor Kimber nodded in acknowledgement, gathered up the sheets and spread out another batch.

'The Council,' said Sebastian. 'I mean, who's to say they get it right, anyway? I mean, just because the councillors are all old and have been to college and stuff, it doesn't mean they know best, does it?'

Councillor Kimber flicked him a very sharp glance.

'I'm afraid it's the best we can do, apprentice.'

'Huh,' said Sebastian.

The divining rods weighed heavy in his hands. When Sebastian ran his thumbnails along them he could just feel the edges of the pressure-plates.

Mr Meeno was a great man, there was no doubt about that. And that man who had been campaigning against the casino: well, the accident with the runaway mincer had certainly caused the poor man a great deal of inconvenience, not to mention disfigurement, but it was probably no more than an accident.

Mr Meeno was a complete genius. He'd fixed it so he could make up any law he wanted and there was no one to stop him. At least, someone would stop him in the end, when people got mad enough. That was why Mr Meeno was taking things gradually. What was it he'd said? Oh yes: "We cannot afford to overload the system, here." That meant there couldn't be too many laws thrown out too quickly, or someone, like Councillor Kimber, say, would take action.

Suddenly, Sebastian thought again about the High Priest's face, wobbly with terror, and he knew what he had to do.

He waited until he saw a paper that bore the crest of the Education Department and then he pressed hard with his thumbs.

Councillor Kimber jumped as if someone had stuck a pin into him.

'It's impossible,' he said, in a puff. 'Intolerable! Quite, absolutely intolerable!' He snatched up the offending sheet and scanned it hastily.

'Schools,' he muttered. 'That could be worse, I suppose.'

'Hm,' said Turville and went off to find a copy of the

Sacred Texts.

By the time Turville returned Councillor Kimber was waving the sheet of paper in the air.

'There can't be anything wrong with *this*,' he exclaimed, a little wildly. 'Ora can't object to an increase in the number of toilets available for each class of children, surely!'

'Well –' began Sebastian, but then fortunately had an inspiration. 'Perhaps it's not something actually to do with that,' he said. 'Perhaps it's something quite different. Perhaps it's that you've missed something out of your laws and Ora, well, He's just telling you. Perhaps there's something extra that you're supposed to do at the same time as putting in all the extra toilets.'

Councillor Kimber was looking at Sebastian as if he'd grown horns.

'Something extra? *Something extra*?'

'Like ... like hot-air driers or something,' said Sebastian.

'Ooh,' said Turville, 'I don't like those. They just blow the germs around, they do and they take all the oil out of your hands. I've taken to carrying some hand cream around with me, just in case. There's a lovely one you can get in the stores: Jasmine Quest, it's called and–'

'Yes, yes, yes, no doubt,' said Councillor Kimber, hurriedly. 'What do the texts actually say, apprentice?'

Sebastian let the book gently fall open. He found himself reading the passage they'd been reading earlier:

'... by your power I have arms and legs and probably on a good day the patience to do it. It seems right that I should use the gifts that I have been given ...'

Sebastian found Councillor Kimber looking over his shoulder.

'Ora can't be asking us to put textured plaster up in the toilets, surely!' said Councillor Kimber, wildly. 'And as for a clockwork spit–'

'Hm,' said Sebastian. It was a useful noise, that suggested deep consideration with just a touch of limitless wisdom and it passed the time while he wondered what on earth he could do. 'Yes, I see. Yes, it's not so much that this law is wrong, it's more that there's a law you haven't made.'

Councillor Kimber looked from the Sacred Texts to the pages of law with bulging eyes.

'A new law we haven't made?'

'That's right. Ah, I see the connection, now: it's about ... about everybody having arms and legs.'

Councillor Kimber threw his arms up in the air.

'It's Ora's will that everybody should have arms and legs? Well, really, apprentice –'

'Nah,' said Sebastian, hastily. 'Course not. Everybody knows that. No, it's about everyone using their arms and legs. Of course, when Ora did that law about the teachers doing keep-fit and stuff we should have put the children in, too.'

'All the children should have keep-fit classes,' repeated Councillor Kimber, with a dangerous edge to his voice.

'No. No, keep-fit's not much fun, is it? No. Football. You see, Ora's just saying, if you're making the toilets bigger, then there's still got to be plenty of changing rooms so people can change for football.'

Councillor Kimber began walking backwards and forwards very fast.

'But children in schools have always played football,' he said, with an effort at calmness.

'Yeah, but not enough football. You see, everybody in school has to play football all afternoon. Every day.'

Councillor Kimber swung round on Sebastian, head down, like a bull about to charge.

'Everybody in schools ...' he growled.

'That's right. Except the girls, obviously,' Sebastian added, hastily. 'Girls aren't much good at football. They squeal if the ball goes near them and they get upset if they get their boots muddy. No, the girls must use their arms and legs to ... er ... to do cooking. That's it. Lots of cooking, especially cakes and buns and pies and stuff. All right?'

Councillor Kimber made a squawking noise.

'You're expecting me to go back to the Council and tell them ...'

'Oh, and biscuits,' said Sebastian.

Councillor Kimber walked round in a circle several times and then swung back to Sebastian, red-faced, breathing slowly, his fury only just barely controlled.

'You know this is serious, don't you?' he said. 'I know the people on the Council seem very old and dull to you, but that doesn't mean they'll just sit there and take this. There have been arguments already. People are getting angry. Do you understand?'

'Yeah,' said Sebastian. 'Course.'

'So, apprentice, *are you sure that this is the will of Ora*?'

Sebastian took a deep breath and thought about Mr Meeno and about how he'd filled up the system to capacity for some time, now and he found himself filled with a new confidence.

'Well, I wouldn't take a chance on something like that, would I?' said Sebastian, putting his hands behind his back so he could cross his fingers. 'Not when it was a question of the will of Ora. I mean, what could Ora do to me if I did something He didn't like? He could blast me right out of existence. Make me feel as though someone had put a red-hot poker inside me. Make my arms and legs rot away and drop off. Melt my eyeballs so they run right down my–'

'Quite,' said Councillor Kimber, suddenly weary. 'Well, may Ora bless us all, apprentice. Because I am very much afraid that we are all going to need it.'

Turville came back and looked carefully at Sebastian once he'd shown Councillor Kimber out.

'I've never heard of Ora melting anyone's eyeballs,' he said.

'No,' said Sebastian. 'Of course not. Ora would never do a thing like that, would He? But He could.'

'Really,' said Turville.

'If He wanted to,' said Sebastian.

Sebastian went to see Gerald, to tell him all about it, but Gerald was lying in his nest and when Sebastian stroked him, to wake him up, all Gerald did was push a pink and feebly quivering nose out through the sawdust and then snuggle back wearily and go back to sleep.

Chapter 27

The statue of Ora was actually in the way, a bit, if you were putting on a big show complete with dancers in high heels, plumes and toothpaste smiles.

Sebastian waited until the crashing chords at the end of the big number, did a cartwheel off the offering podium and announced, 'That's all, folks!' into the mike. There was a happy spatter of applause from the offerers, which was quelled instantly by the deadly eyebrows of the vergers and then Sebastian stuck his hands in his pockets and went to have a mooch round the shop.

When you hung about behind the postcard stand you heard all sorts of things.

'Worth seeing, hey?' said someone. 'Real live-wire, that apprentice!'

'You're telling me. Have you seen the fireworks? We were here the day the Women's Congress banner caught fire and the kids were thrilled to bits to see all the vergers tottering about with fire extinguishers.'

'May I help you?'

Sebastian hastily ducked down under the nearest book display unit. That cut-glass voice belonged to Mrs Poash.

'Just this postcard of the apprentice, thank you.'

There was a sniff almost sharp enough to do heart

surgery with.

'It's for my granddaughter's bedroom, I want it. She's taken quite a shine to that one, since he was on *Celebrity Knocks*.'

'Just like my grandson,' said a woman's voice. 'He just loves the new football law, my grandson does: can't wait to get to school and that makes a change. Always was a fidget, that one. Like most boys.'

'The large number of children now visiting the Temple is causing a great deal of mess and disruption,' said Mrs Poash, severely. 'There's one boy in particular upon whom I have to keep a very close eye.'

'Well, these things are sent to try us,' said someone.

'That's right. Like this casino business,' said someone else. 'Odd, Ora wanting something like that right outside the Temple. And having them knock down the old Council Chamber, too. Sad, that was. Makes you wonder what's coming next, doesn't it?'

'We must submit to the will of Ora,' said Mrs Poash, piously.

'Yes. Well, we don't have a lot of choice about that, do we, ma'am?'

'No,' said Mrs Poash and suddenly her tone was bleak. 'No, we don't.'

Sebastian waited until the coast was clear and then crawled

out from between the bookshelves. There was a small girl with a runny nose watching him.

'What?' said Sebastian, but not unkindly.

'Is it allowed to go in there?' she asked.

'It is for me,' said Sebastian. 'I was wondering about ... er ... putting little robots in the bookshelves. So that when you pick a book up, it says "Ora wants you for a sunflower."'

She sniffed. It wasn't as cutting a sniff as Mrs Poash's, but it was going to get there before she got much bigger.

'What are you wearing a dress for?'

Sebastian scowled, but she only put her head on one side to get the hair out of her eyes, and carried on staring.

'It's not a dress,' explained Sebastian. 'It's my sacred robe. It's because I'm the High Priest's apprentice, I am.'

'Oh. Are you the one that bungee-jumped down from the roof and then let all the doves fly round the dome?'

'Yeah.'

'Oh.' A huge blissful smile split her small face. 'One of the doves *went* on Great-Auntie Rita.'

Sebastian puffed out his chest.

'Takes skill, getting them to do that,' he said. 'Especially on great-aunts. You have to train them to recognize the silly hats.'

She gazed at him some more, critically.

'Ora chose you.'

'Yep.'

She shrugged a little, as if at something beyond understanding.

'He must like you ever so ever so much, then,' she said.

'Yep,' said Sebastian. 'Yeah. Well, He would do, wouldn't He?'

Sebastian stopped on his way back to his quarters, looking up past the great shining thighs to the deep tiger-stone eyes of the god of the City.

'Hey,' he muttered, 'I know you wouldn't really do anything about the eyeballs, all right?'

And he went in search of Bert, who was taking him to the Grand Theatre to watch a rehearsal of the new play. Sebastian enjoyed the play immensely, particularly as they let him be Colonel Blunder. It was true that the colonel was shot in the first five minutes, but his body proved to be an important part of the proceedings, falling out of cupboards and lying under sofa cushions in the most thrilling manner. And it was great fun to see the leading lady having huge hysterics when it was discovered that the murder weapon had somehow been loaded with live ammunition. It might have been quite nasty if the script hadn't called for the first shot to be fired into the air and even so, it nearly winged a lighting man.

'Not to worry,' said Sebastian. 'That sort of thing happens all the time.'

'Does it?' asked the director, as white as dough.

'Well, it does to me,' said Sebastian.

Chapter 28

There were cranes on the Holy Hill. Sebastian noticed them as he drove home on Saturday. 'It's for the casino,' explained Bert. 'Surprising Ora went for that. If you ask me, it's going to be a terrible eyesore. Still, it's the word of Ora. And, as Mrs Poash always says, all we can do is make Him offerings and pray that He will be merciful.'

'Yeah,' said Sebastian. 'Well, He always is, isn't He?'

Bert glanced up at his mirror and smiled.

'You're a good lad,' he said. 'I expect it'll all work out, however barmy it seems.' He began to laugh. 'My youngest, he's as pleased as punch about these new football laws. Plays all afternoon he does and he loves it.'

In the plush dimness of the limo, Sebastian smirked.

Robert was less than pleased about the extra football, though and Edward was furious. Sebastian sat peacefully while they ranted on, but they were nothing to Eunice, when she got home. She kicked the door open violently and came in balancing three plastic food boxes under her chin.

Robert and Edward perked up.

'What is it today?' asked Edward. 'Cake?'

Eunice shot the boxes a look of vitriolic loathing.

'Honey and sultana flapjacks,' she said, with a hiss of

disgust. 'Made with butter. *Death* just waiting to happen!'

Edward looked pleased.

'May I have one?' he asked.

Eunice threw a box on the table in front of him.

'You can have the lot if you like,' she muttered and then went to hurl the rest into the sink.

Edward, unusually pink, went and got three plates out of the cupboard.

The flapjacks were glistening with stickiness. Robert peered in, counting.

'I suppose we'd better leave one for Dad,' he said, regretfully.

'And I suppose Mum might like one.'

'Two each, then.'

Edward pursed his lips disapprovingly.

'You'd better not have two, Robert. Think of the cholesterol. Think of the sugar. And the calories.'

'True,' said Robert, through a blissful mouthful. 'But think of all that exercise we've had this afternoon, hurtling round after a football. I reckon I need an energy boost. Are you sure you don't want one, Eunice?'

Eunice's hiss was almost a spit.

'You must be joking. I have just spent a whole lesson making those things. A whole lesson! Here I am studying for my Terminals and what happens? They pass some idiotic law and I end up faffing about half the day with honey and oat flakes!'

Robert carefully selected the largest remaining flapjack.

'It can't be an idiotic law,' he pointed out. 'Not if it's the will of Ora.'

'Anyway, I don't know what you're moaning about,' said Edward. 'At least you get an end product: all you get from football is bruised, muddy and shouted at.'

Robert looked suspiciously at Sebastian.

'Do you have to play football?' he asked.

'Oh. Yeah. Course,' said Sebastian, for that was the juiciest part of the whole thing. 'I mean, it's the will of Ora, isn't it?'

'But who do you play with? Not the vergers, do you?'

Sebastian couldn't help but smile. He couldn't play all afternoon, because of Offerings, but he more than made up for it in Quality Time.

'Golden United,' he said and Robert and Edward both went quite quite green.

Yeah. So far, even with Mr Meeno in the equation, things were working out all right.

Mr Walty held the Sacred Texts away from him at a readable distance.

'Ah,' he said. 'Yes. Today we have another crime story.'

'Cor, brilliant,' said Sebastian. 'I bet it was the butler. Or the mysterious scarred stranger. With a banana, in the bathroom.'

'With a banana?'

'Yeah. Well, a *lead* banana, painted so it looks like –'

'Just listen, Blewitt,' said Mr Walty.

One day Ora was walking in the City when He saw an overturned wagon, and a young man lying lifeless on the ground beside it. And there was another young man there, also, with a driving whip in his hand. And Ora was angry, and He said: 'By your recklessness, you have destroyed life, which is the fruit of my breath, so now you shall lose your own.' But the young man fell on his face before Ora, and he said: 'Be merciful, great god. I am a fool, but I am also the fruit of Your breath.'

And Ora wept, and He said: 'Then, shall I make the universe perfect again?'

And the great tears of Ora pierced the heart of the young man, and he wept also.

So Ora called together several of the wisest people in the City, and said to them: 'Rule the city as best you may, for I cannot act here.'

But they, being wise, doubted their own wisdom; so Ora said: 'I will give you a sign.' And He gave them golden divining rods that told His will; and by that they found courage and strength and comfort.

And so the City lived in peace and prospered mightily.

And though Ora was seldom seen in the City, the people held Him in their hearts, and they sang:

'Sweet is the gift of Ora, freely given.
Warm is the love of Ora, which leaves us free.
Great is the hand of Ora, but light as air.'

Chapter 29

The sun shone with undimmed splendour. The City had always been remarkable for its glorious weather and its sun-rebounding golden walls were famous for casting a glow of beauty on every face.

Not that you noticed it much, with some people: Finley Wortle's face was getting so long it would almost have fitted in a drainpipe and Councillor Kimber, who had never looked sunny to start with, was stalking the City like a dyspeptic ghoul. He was quoted as saying: 'My faith in Ora is unchanged'; though it was known that several of the Council were having grave doubts about the wisdom of the City's being governed by a non-elected god. At least the new security man Councillor Kimber had had stationed by the main entrance gave old Finley someone to talk to, which was nice, although, actually, Finley had picked up one or two supporters just lately. Sometimes, when someone opened the main door, you could hear them protesting.

The papers ran large headlines about all the troubles and there were Letters to the Editor, but mostly people carried on turning straight to the back pages for the sport. And, generally, except for the sad death of dear old

Crispin Carter, the ancient polo champion and career criminal, under the wheel of a runaway milk float; and a mysterious spate of people hand-cuffing themselves to the main-line; and the curious incident where someone installed a telegraph wire just at throat height halfway down the huge new flume at the aquadome, which might have hurt Sebastian quite badly if they hadn't sent a dummy down first as a demonstration, things were generally peaceful.

Sebastian kept himself busy working on some new Offerings routines. It was worth going, people said, just to see the show. If it wasn't the jazz band, it might be the ventriloquist and if it wasn't the ventriloquist it might be the poetic parrots, the sword-swallower, the formation abseiling, the creation of the world in synchronized football skills, or the giant origami team that conjured up a whole forest that you were allowed to take home afterwards. And, even if you were unlucky and got the moose-head folk dancers or the Vergers' Dramatic Society, then there was always a chance that the apprentice might pop up in the middle of it and tell a few jokes.

Then one Sunday Sebastian came back from a visit home to find his burglar alarm blinking anxiously from inside his bedside cupboard. That meant the High Priest had had a night-time visit from somebody. Sebastian re-set the alarm, which he had programmed with extreme care *not* to ring and waited to find out what was going to happen next.

What happened was: firstly, the High Priest stopped singing for several days; secondly, the next time Councillor Kimber bustled dourly along he was ushered straight in to see the High Priest himself; and, thirdly, Councillor Kimber was dark with clouds of storming fury when he swirled out.

The High Priest's new law was announced in four-inch letters on the front page of every newspaper. Sebastian couldn't see what all the fuss was about, to start with: it just said that everyone in the police had to have a day off for training every week. Well, so what? After all, it was remarkable how *old* policemen always looked: there might be ones who didn't know what a mobile phone was, or a maxi-disc.

Then Sebastian read a bit further and discovered that the police training days were Fridays and even Sebastian could see that all the police going off duty for a whole day a week might cause problems.

It was such a completely daft idea that no one quite believed it for several days; even the papers treated it as a bit of a joke. The only person who took it really seriously from the beginning was Councillor Kimber. He visited the High Priest every day for a week and got more doom-laden and furious with each visit. Sebastian felt quite excited: Mr Meeno was obviously planning some big crime and Sebastian looked forward very much to seeing what would happen.

The first thing that happened on the next Friday was that the milkman didn't show up.

'I'm not surprised,' said Turville, quite ruffled, 'really I'm not. Who would want to risk going out? People are afraid, Your Knowingness.'

Mr Walty didn't show up, either. He phoned to say that Mrs Walty was rather nervous, so he thought he'd better stay at home.

Sebastian and Gerald sat and watched the telly. The reporters were terribly agitated: there were huge tailbacks on all major routes because of accidents; people were staying away from work; the old people were in fear of their lives. The reporters were particularly frustrated because they kept wanting to interview policemen and of course there weren't any available.

There was a huge crowd of people at Offerings that afternoon, but the whole thing was strangely subdued. It was true that there wasn't much of a show, because the formation poodles hadn't turned up for fear of dognappers, but no one in the congregation even went 'Whooh!' when Sebastian did a perfect cartwheel that landed him exactly at the Place of Offering (and it was generally difficult to stop tourists, especially from the Western States, going 'Whooh!'). And when Sebastian looked down at the faces of all the people, gold in the light from the little inlaid mirrors on the gilded pillars, they looked anxious and pinched.

He vaulted down from the podium and went and stood between the calves of the great statue of Ora.

'It's all right,' he said. 'Honestly. Look, the Temple and everything's here just the same. Ora's here, too. Everything's going to be all right.'

And a sigh rose up from the people and filled the dome.

There were a lot of offerings that afternoon: it was almost as if people thought that making an offering would make Ora protect them from burglars and muggers. It was all a bit silly, really: but when the Temple was shutting for the night Sebastian stopped just for a moment before the great golden statue with its all-seeing eyes.

'Here,' he muttered. 'Help me look after that lot, all right?'

The papers next morning had five-inch headlines:

CITY WITHOUT CRIME

they said. Sebastian read it all out to Gerald while they

had their morning trifle. In the whole twenty-four hours of the police training day there had been no reported crime whatsoever.

'Isn't it wonderful,' said Turville, tripping in. 'It's such a good thing it's all passed off so peacefully. People have been getting just so upset, over the past few days, it's been breaking my heart to see them and the poor High Priest is just *devastated*.'

Sebastian helped himself to another chocolate mint.

'People were really frightened, yesterday,' he said.

Turville waggled his shoulders.

'And it's not just that, Your Knowingness. They're discontented,' he said. 'I mean, we get more people in here in one day than we used to get in a week, but there's a restlessness about. It's as if . . . as if they're losing their trust. They're all talking about modern governments and how the City should be ruled for the good of the people. It's as if they've forgotten what the Temple and Ora are all about. Still, at least dear Finley has got some company, poor man. Now, what will you have to drink, Your Knowingness? Maple-syrup double-thick chocolate-swirl milk shake, as usual, or a cup of tea?'

'Er ... tea, I think.'

'Won't be a tick.'

Sebastian sipped his tea and discovered that he was a bit disappointed. Mr Meeno had arranged this police day-off thing and Sebastian had been extremely interested to see what big crime Mr Meeno had been planning to pull off while it was in force. But now nothing had happened. Why not?

Turville came in with the post.

'Seven fan letters, Your Knowingness and a parcel.'

Sebastian held out his hand and then suddenly hesitated.

'Is it heavy?' he asked. 'You know, like that one that exploded?'

'Oh, no, Your Knowingness. I've put it through the X-ray machine and there's nothing metal in it apart from a paper-clip.'

Sebastian opened it, but it was just a bundle of newspaper cuttings. There was a picture of him standing in the portico just about where that beehive vase had fallen. And there was one of him coming down from the dome on the zip-wire–the one that had snapped and would have sent him falling to his death if it hadn't been for him bouncing off all the helium balloons that had been blown up ready for the flying guinea pigs, so he'd ended up safely on the clown's rubber motorbike.

In fact, now he looked back, he'd had quite a few

narrow escapes. There were the falling speakers that had nearly got Gerald and that poisonous pizza that they'd only discovered because it had turned the knife green. And that exploding cake. At the time it'd seemed quite natural that someone had got their ingredients muddled up and used high explosive instead of marzipan, but ... There were other strange things, too, now he looked back: like the time the steering on the carnival truck got stuck and they'd been lucky to end up in a ditch with their mouths full of airbag rather than crashing through the central reservation of the motorway . . . and the time he'd gone to visit the Reptile House for a chat with the keepers and they discovered a deadly and very highly-strung shaker snake in a tank that should only have contained Ambrose, the amber chameleon.

It was all very odd: and so was the fact that he'd so often caught a glimpse of an ugly pale face and an oily fringe as he'd gone about the place. And he hadn't been imagining it, because Mrs Poash was always going on about Sebastian's little friend coming along all by himself to visit the Temple.

Horace, that was.

Horace Meeno.

So: was it Mr Meeno who wanted Sebastian out of the way? Surely a kind man like Mr Meeno wouldn't want to do a thing like that, would he? Or was it only Horace?

Whoever it was, it might be an idea if Sebastian was harder to damage when he went out into the City.

He asked Turville to get him a suit of armour.

Chapter 30

The next couple of weeks passed: Sebastian went on army manoeuvres, saw a rather dull film at the cinema for which he was officially too young, took the controls on a passenger jet as it was coming into land at the airport, went on the Death-Frenzy ride at Glitter Towers fifteen times without having to queue and had five candyflosses in one afternoon without being sick. Ill-luck – if it was ill-luck – continued to haunt him. The cinema caught fire, for instance and they were lucky to avoid a mid-air collision after someone's mobile jammed the air traffic control system. There was nothing wrong with the candyfloss: but that might have been because Sebastian was careful not to have any from the recommended stall.

Even the Fridays passed: the postman didn't come, it was true, and it was almost impossible to buy petrol, and there were tales of gangs who went about shouting and banging on doors and breaking windows and frightening people. But then there were also lots of new jobs for security guards. Even so, several protest meetings were arranged, especially after the unfortunate incident in which three tourists were mugged in the

Temple square.

Councillor Kimber was photographed directing the traffic after the digging for the casino brought the whole East Circular to a graunching halt.

The Council itself had gone on strike completely, which meant that it had stopped sending laws to the Temple. Sebastian, not sure whether to be disappointed or pleased, shelved his plans for banning rat-catchers throughout the City and continued to keep a sharp eye out for rampaging pneumatic drills and scorpions in his slippers. The High Priest was still seldom to be seen. Turville was worried about him: apparently he was very unhappy, and spending a lot of time in prayer.

Of course Eunice and Robert and Edward were hugely passionate about the whole business, though Sebastian knew better than to listen to them. This was partly from experience–if he'd listened to that lot yakking on he'd have gone mad long ago–and partly because he had other things on his mind.

He was worried about Gerald.

It was nothing sudden, nothing obvious. Gerald might have been off his food a bit, but then so had Sebastian, lately and so it had seemed quite natural. There was just a subtle loss of condition. Gerald's coat lost its superb shine and had begun to look a bit patchy. He no longer scrabbled at the walls of his run when Sebastian went to see him. He stopped climbing tablecloths, too and he seemed unhappy to sit on Sebastian's shoulder.

'Do you think he's all right?' Sebastian asked Turville, one day. Gerald was sitting, rather hunched and he looked irritable, not his usual self at all.

'Well, he's eaten all his chocolate drops, hasn't he, Your Knowingness? So there can't be much wrong, can there?'

Sebastian felt a bit more hopeful, but another proper look at Gerald dispelled that hope. Gerald's black eyes were no longer shining and eager; his whiskers were no longer trembling with intelligence.

'He doesn't *look* very happy,' said Sebastian, carefully, because only old or stupid people worried.

Turville looked at Gerald again and shook his head.

'I don't know much about sickness,' he said. 'There was a Temple cat, once: a lovely marmalade, he was. I know we had a terrible job clipping his claws.'

'I don't think Gerald's very well,' said Sebastian, tremendously off-handedly.

He reached out a finger to stroke Gerald, but Gerald gave no sign of pleasure at all. It was as if he hardly noticed. Sebastian felt a rising tide of anxiety, but he leant casually back in his chair so it wouldn't show.

'Oh dear,' said Turville, regarding Gerald carefully. 'You've got me quite worried, now, Your Knowingness. Gerald's a real little character, isn't he?'

Gerald wasn't looking much of a character. His splendid sleekness and enthusiasm had vanished. He looked morose.

'He doesn't seem quite himself,' said Sebastian.

'Well ... then perhaps he ought to see a vet, Your Knowingness.'

A vet? Gerald wasn't ill enough to need a vet. But perhaps he could have a check-over. A sort of rat MOT.

'Perhaps you could make him an appointment sometime,' said Sebastian, quietly.

'Very well, Your Knowingness.'

'I'm sure it's nothing, really. But perhaps they'll have one for today, just to be sure.'

'I'm sure they'd be happy to make time for Gerald, Your Knowingness.'

'Yeah. Do you think you could ring up now?'

'Very well, Your Knowingness.'

'And tell Bert to bring the car round, will you?'

Chapter 31

Turville found Sebastian some ordinary clothes to change into. They felt strange after his heavy gold-embroidered robes, but Turville said it might cause a fuss if it got about that there was a rat living in the Temple.

'People can be really funny about things like that,' he said.

They left the limo behind and Bert gave them a lift down in his own car. They had to go the long way round because of the diversions around the casino site. Gerald didn't seem to enjoy the ride: his claws slipped on the cardboard of his box and he spent most of his time cowering down in one corner.

The waiting room was lined with battered chairs and most of them were full.

'Ah,' said the receptionist, running her pen down the appointments register. 'Gerald and Mr Turville. Do sit down for a moment.'

Sebastian hadn't waited for anything for ages, but Turville led them to a couple of chairs in a corner. Sebastian sat down with Gerald's box clutched to him.

'What have you got there?' asked a cheerful old man with a mongrel on a string.

'A rat,' said Sebastian. 'A real wild brown one. Only

he's tamed, now, of course.'

The old man nodded and grinned.

'I had a rat when I was your age,' he said. 'Nice animal, he was. Very clean. Very particular, rats are, I've found.'

'Amazing, isn't it,' said Turville. 'You always hear that they're dirty creatures, but this one's a treasure.'

Gerald was exploring his box. It tipped suddenly as he pattered from one end to the other. Sebastian held it extra firmly: the old man's mongrel was showing signs of interest.

'I've seen you somewhere before.' An upright lady with a cloth-covered cage was staring at him accusingly. 'Yes, I know you from somewhere.'

'I don't think so,' said Sebastian, gratefully, because she looked as sour as crab-apples.

'I'll tell you who he reminds me of,' said the old man, suddenly, 'and that's the new apprentice. Coo, he isn't half a live wire, he is. My little grandchildren, they're always pestering me to take them to the Temple to make an offering and to see the granny-ballet, or the monocycling. Nice, it is, that he's doing something for the young people.'

'My kids like the balloon animals best,' said a man with a goldfish. 'That and the singing squirrels.'

The lady's face had curdled with distaste.

'Personally,' she said, 'it grieves me greatly that the

solemn atmosphere of the Temple of Ora has been made into a mockery by cheap and vulgar theatricals!'

'Tweety and Mrs Bagg!' said the receptionist and the lady got frostily to her feet.

'It's the budgie I feel sorry for,' said the old man, as the door closed behind her.

Sebastian was glad that people were enjoying the offering shows, but he did have to admit that there was something extra special about the Temple in the evenings, when it had closed for the night. That was when he really felt Ora listening, just as Mrs Poash preferred to talk to Him in the early mornings. Now he came to think about it, Mrs Poash had been a bit chirpier, lately. What he'd do, Sebastian decided, was to organize a quiet hour every day before Offerings. Then, all the people who wanted to talk to Ora quietly could do so before the show started. Yeah. That'd be no trouble.

'Gerald and Mr Turville!'

'Ah, lovely,' said Turville, beaming. 'Marvellous. Thank you so much.'

The man in the next room wore a thin white coat over a tweed jacket and he seemed to be in a hurry.

'Mr Turville? Good morning. Right. What do we have here?'

'A rat,' Sebastian told him. 'He's called Gerald.' Sebastian watched anxiously as the vet lifted the lid off

Gerald's box. Gerald was sitting sullenly in a corner. His whiskers were drooping.

'Goodness me,' said the vet stepping back rather hurriedly. 'Don't often see a brown fellow like him.'

'He's a wild rat,' Sebastian explained.

'Yes, so I see. And how did you come by him, then?'

'I found him when he was a baby,' said Sebastian and explained all about it.

The vet had relaxed considerably by the end of the story.

'So he's quite tame?'

'Well, he's still a proper wild rat: he can forage for his food and everything. Only he's not seemed so well, lately, so we brought him in.'

The vet peered at Gerald closely and then slipped in an experienced hand and lifted Gerald out onto the table. Gerald, very cowed, pressed himself down as close to the table as he could. The vet stroked him from nose to tail, picked him up and looked at his claws, inspected his eyes and nose and mouth and tail and Gerald looked hideously undignified and embarrassed.

'What do you feed him on?' asked the vet, at last.

'Super-rambo rat food,' said Turville, 'from the pet stall in the market place.'

'I see. And what else?'

Sebastian shifted uneasily, remembering the chocolate

drops and the biscuits and the cake. And the saucers of cream. And eggs.

'He comes out for exercise twice every day,' he said. 'But he does scavenge a bit.'

The vet ran his hands down Gerald's sides and Gerald flinched.

'Well, it's a good thing for him to get plenty of exercise,' the vet said, lifting Gerald, splay-footed with terror, back into the box. 'But I'm afraid the scavenging has got to stop.'

'Oh,' said Sebastian, watching a shrinking Gerald scuttling over to push his nose into a corner of his box.

'What you have there,' said the vet, peering severely at Sebastian over his glasses, 'is an extremely unhealthy rat. And the reason he's unhealthy, Master ... er ... Turville, is because he's very fat – and that's bad for him in all sorts of ways. You'll have noticed, I expect, that his coat's lost condition. That he's not as lively as he used to be.'

Sebastian nodded, overcome with remorse. He'd been giving Gerald all that extra food without even thinking about whether it was good for him and now Gerald was suffering.

'He needs to change his diet immediately,' said the vet, briskly, washing his hands. 'Switch him to a basic rat food with not too many oily seeds in it. And, if you want to give him treats, let him have a bit of cucumber or apple, or perhaps a bit of dry crust. And only water to drink. I think you'll soon see him pick up, then. All right? If you'll pay at the desk. Good day to you, then.'

They were all very quiet on the way back to the Temple and Mr Walty asked Sebastian twice during lessons if he was feeling all right.

Turville came and hovered in the doorway at lunchtime.

'What will you have for lunch?' he asked. 'Double chips with mayonnaise, as usual? Custard or cream with your treacle pudding?'

Sebastian hesitated. Curiously enough, he felt a bit off chips, but then he had had them pretty well every day for several weeks, now, so he was probably just bored with them. And there was Gerald to think of.

'I think I'll have a change,' he said. 'How about a bowl of tomato soup with some bread to dunk. And perhaps a banana for afters.'

'Ooh, that does sound nice,' said Turville. 'Only the soup will have to be out of a tin, or else you'll have to wait all day for it. We've got some lovely bread, though.'

The scent of tomato soup wafted at Sebastian in a fragrant memory.

'It's brilliant out of the tin,' he said and it was. Gerald was surprised to discover the table wasn't belly-deep in chocolate drops and biscuits. He sniffed round a bit in a way he hadn't done for days and when Turville had the idea of emptying the crumbs from the breadboard over the table, Gerald actually went round, whiskers twitching and delicately lapped them up.

Chapter 32

Sebastian did his dry ice and Temple gong routine at Offerings that afternoon. The *boings* wobbled back off the pillars and expanded into the dome and it was all deeply satisfying, especially the very last *boing*, when he lowered the biggest gong into a huge glass tank of orangeade. The only trouble with the gong show was that it tended to frighten the small children, but Sebastian had got over this by arranging a special puppet show in the chapter house on gong days. Only one child cried and that was when its mother said it was time to go home, so Sebastian chalked up that idea as yet another success.

There were plenty of offerings and a baby that its family wanted to call Petunia Iolanthe Gertrude Perkins.

'What?' said Sebastian. '*Petunia?*'

The baby's mother and father exchanged unhappy glances.

'After her great-aunts,' explained the father, apologetically and the three old ladies hanging around behind him like inverted vampire bats snickered with extreme smugness.

'Huh,' said Sebastian. 'Haven't you got *any* sense? No one's called Petunia these days. Or Iolanthe. Or Gertrude: that's just for really old ladies.'

The great-aunts all went the ugliest shade of confounded purple.

'Can't you think of something better?' asked Sebastian.

The baby's mother whispered something urgently.

'Well ... we did think of Clara,' admitted the father. 'Clara Jane Perkins, that would be.'

'Much better,' said Sebastian. 'Clara Jane Perkins it is. Ta. Thanks a lot. Cheerio, then. Have a nice party.'

And he felt he'd had a successful afternoon.

Sebastian cut a slice of apple into small pieces and hid them in various cunning places round the room. Gerald was slow and still worryingly waddly, but he sniffed them out. He even tipped his head over so that Sebastian could tickle him behind the ear.

'I think he looks a bit better,' said Sebastian, cautiously.

'Oh, yes, Your Knowingness,' said Turville. 'You know, I really think he does.'

That evening Sebastian wandered into the Temple. He wanted to see if he could work out any improvements to the high-wire act. It was ever so popular, but people at the front couldn't always see what was going on. He climbed up the bouncing ladder to the platform and looked down and down to the little gilded pews far below him.

Of course, it was obvious from here: the wire should

run the other way across the dome. That would make it much better.

Sebastian took a careful step onto the wire for a moment. Yes, he was almost sure he could do it: his balance had really improved since he'd got his unicycle. He was going to be brilliant on his skates by the time the river froze over.

Sebastian stepped back onto the platform and slid down the ladder, using the sides of his feet against the rails of the ladder to brake his descent. He hit the floor neatly, bowed to an imaginary audience and made for the cupboard behind the new toddlers' play-hive where he kept his notebook.

He'd move the high wire, as he'd decided and he'd find out about putting a gold confetti shower in, as well. Mind you, the vergers would moan like mad about all the picking up. So–well, perhaps they could use cornflakes, instead: and then the doves could clear up for them. Brilliant!

Sebastian got out his golden key and went to the cupboard. He fitted the key in the lock, turned it and pulled open the door.

It was dim in the evening light of the Temple, so he didn't realize at once what he was looking at. He only sort-of thought *What are those two shiny things?*

And he only thought that for a moment.

There was a slight movement in the darkness of

the cupboard. Sebastian caught a glimpse of a scaly triangular head – and a forked tongue – and –

He acted purely on instinct: he threw himself backwards as far and as fast as he could.

He hit the polished floor with a *thunk* that made every bone in his spine yelp in protest and then he bounced, *thunk!* again and skidded full-length backwards until, with a clash of golden offering bells, he went head first into the marble speaking steps.

He lay and watched the stars spinning past his nose for several moments.

Around him dust sighed and settled elegantly.

All sorts of parts of him were beginning to hurt in really persistent ways, so he tried them out one at a time to find out if they were still attached.

Back: *ouch!* But probably not broken. Elbow: somehow both numb and painful, but just about bendable. Head: muffled and ringing and smarting like blazes at the same time.

He put a wavery hand up to his head. It was too tender to feel much, but the collision with the speaking steps seemed to have created a long graze that had cut a channel through the hair on the top of his head. What ...

That scaly head, the forked tongue and the shining

jet-black eyes.

Good grief.

Good grief!

Sebastian hauled himself in stages to his feet and tottered towards his locker. He stopped a little way away and listened.

Silence.

And then more silence.

And then a long, low rattle.

Good grief.

Sebastian went and got one of the vergers' staves and then, still staggering a little, he used it to push the door on the locker closed.

Then made his way back towards his quarters.

As he passed the great statue of Ora he felt its eyes on him and he stopped.

'Yeah,' he said. 'Look, thanks, all right? And thanks for letting me know about Gerald, too.'

And then he walked quickly away.

That Friday, someone came into the Temple and sprayed red paint on the statue of Ora. The vergers grabbed him almost straightaway and frog-marched him out, but of course he couldn't be arrested, because all the police were on training. The man stood in the doorway and shouted jagged, ugly things that clattered against the pillars of the Temple. Sebastian was doing lessons at the time, but Turville was extremely upset, even though the paint had come off Ora's golden legs with no trouble at all.

'Poor soul,' he said soberly. 'He was so angry and so afraid. He said people were out to get him. And he blamed Ora, he did, because of this police business. Oh, it broke my heart to hear him.'

'But Ora's not like that,' said Sebastian. 'Ora's not the sort of person to do mean things like that. Ora listens to people, that's all. It's because He likes us.'

'Doesn't sound much of a job, being a god, when you put it like that,' said Turville.

'But everybody knows that,' said Sebastian.

Turville sighed.

'Everybody doesn't,' he said.

Chapter 33

On Tuesday Bert drove Sebastian home in the limo, as usual, sliding effortlessly past the stout stomping figure of Finley and his followers, round the new casino diversions and through the honey-gold streets.

Sebastian let himself in through the back door and the atmosphere in the house hit him like a brick. Eunice was unpacking a cinnamon-smelling pie from a plastic box and Edward was stuffing mud-soaked sports kit into the washing machine.

They both stopped to glare at him.

'What's the matter?' he asked, because his new side-parting completely hid his line of missing hair.

Eunice slammed a wooden spoon into the sink.

'Your precious Sacred Texts, that's what's the matter,' she said, viciously. 'Look at this! Do you know what this is?'

She held the pie only inches from his face, so he had to squint at it.

'It's a pie,' he said and then sniffed, cautiously. 'An apple pie.'

'Yes,' snapped Eunice. 'It's a golden city-style apple pie with grapes and spice and perfect pie pastry.'

'Oh,' said Sebastian and took a step backwards from

Eunice's glittering eyes. 'It looks very nice.'

Eunice slammed it down on the table with almost enough force to break the dish.

'Looks nice? *Looks nice?* I should think it does! Do you know how long it has taken me to make that thing?'

She looked as if she was about to seize Sebastian by the throat, so he took another step backwards.

'Er ... it must have taken ages,' he said.

Eunice's voice rose to a scream.

'It's taken me all afternoon!' she howled. 'Did you hear that? All afternoon! Here I am, in my final year at school and your stupid Sacred Texts say I've got to waste all this time making an apple pie! I don't even like apple pies!'

'But I do,' said Sebastian, reasonably. 'Most people do. And anyway, the Sacred Texts aren't stupid.'

'Cooking's not as stupid as football,' said Edward, sourly. 'At least you can eat apple pies – at least there's an end product. All you get from football is hours of glutinous misery on a bit of half-reclaimed *marshland* and your glasses broken.'

Sebastian had noticed the twist of grubby sticking plaster wrapped round Edward's glasses. It made him look almost human.

'And it won't make any difference to your getting in to university,' Sebastian pointed out. 'I mean, everyone's having to do cooking or football: so you'll all be level, won't you.'

'But ... cooking!' wailed Eunice. 'It's so degrading! Only stupid people cook!'

'Thank you, Eunice,' said Mrs Blewitt, heaving several bags of shopping through the door. 'Hello, Sebastian, darling. How are you?'

'All right,' said Sebastian.

'I didn't mean you, Mummy,' said Eunice, pettishly. 'I'm just feeling very very stressed.'

Mrs Blewitt hoisted each bag carefully up onto the table.

'Aren't we all,' she said. 'Where's Robert?'

'At school,' said Edward. 'He got picked for the football team again. He was furious.'

'Oh, but what an honour,' said Mrs Blewitt, weakly. 'Anyway, Robert quite likes football.'

'Not in his own time,' said Edward. 'He'd much rather be doing something useful, like his Latin homework.'

Sebastian gave up on them all and went out into the backyard.

Two minutes later he was back.

'Where's my football?' he asked. 'And where have you put my goalposts?'

Mrs Blewitt sank down gratefully with her cup of tea.

'I don't think anyone's touched them,' she said. 'Ooh, my feet do ache: it's always such murder at the shops now they all close on Fridays. The queue went right back to the frozen peas.'

Sebastian turned to Edward, who was gloomily scratching bits of mud off the inside of his arm.

'Have you been mucking about with my goalposts?' he demanded.

Edward laughed, wildly, but feebly.

'You must be crazy,' he said. 'If there is one object in the universe I regard with more loathing than a football, it is a set of goalposts. I'm forced to spend an hour and a half every day sinking into the mud between a pair of wooden posts while wild-eyed yobs kick balls at me. The last thing I'm going to do voluntarily is go anywhere near a goalpost.'

'Oh,' said Sebastian, disconcerted. 'Do you think Robert's borrowed them?'

Mrs Blewitt was beginning to look puzzled.

'Have you looked in the shed, darling?'

Sebastian nodded vigorously.

'And are you sure something hasn't been put in front of them?'

'Yeah. Now you've cleared it all out there's nothing left to hide anything behind.'

He suddenly found himself confronted by three open mouths, so it was like looking at the side of a snooker table.

'What?' shrieked Eunice, sitting up straight. 'Someone's cleared out the shed?'

'Oh good heavens,' said Mrs Blewitt, putting down her mug and going quite white.

'Not my encyclopaedias,' whispered Edward, palely. 'Don't tell me my encyclopaedias have gone!'

'Yep,' said Sebastian. 'There aren't any books out there at all now.'

Eunice jerked in horror.

'Not even my bound editions of the Barristers' Gazette?'

'Those green ones we use for propping up the garden table?'

'Yes, yes!'

'The ones in the cardboard box next to the freezer?'

'Yes. Are they still there?'

'Nope. And where have you put the freezer?'

'*Not the freezer*!' cried Mrs Blewitt and jumped up and ran out.

The shed was empty except for Dad's car-mending overalls, which hung limply on the door.

They all stared in.

'Burglars!' said Edward. 'When was the last time anyone came out here?'

They looked at each other.

'Not for ages,' said Eunice.

'Oh dear,' said Mrs Blewitt. 'Let's see. We had turnip crumble last night and at the weekend ... I don't think I've been out here since Friday morning.'

'Friday!' said Edward.

'My books!' said Eunice.

'Huh,' said Sebastian, bitterly. 'What about my goalposts, that's what I want to know! They were good goalposts, they were. They weren't your ordinary wooden goalposts, they were metal. *Non-rusting* metal goalposts.'

'Oh my goodness,' gasped Mrs Blewitt. 'Whatever will Dad say about the lawnmower?'

They all took in sharp breaths at the thought of the anguish to come.

'And – oh no,' said Eunice. 'What about our ice skates?'

They were all struck dumb by this loss. What would they do without their skates? They wouldn't be able to go for rambles along the river at Wassail; they wouldn't be able to join in the festival of sweets.

'And what about all the food I've just bought?' asked Mrs Blewitt. 'It'll all defrost and be spoiled. And there was a whole batch of batter puddings in the freezer and the rest of Dad's runner beans he was so proud of. And some of Eunice's cakes.'

'Blow my cakes,' said Eunice. 'What about dinner?'

They had to eat the things that Mrs Blewitt had just brought from the supermarket: four pounds of sprouts, forty-eight fish fingers and a tub of ice-cream that was supposed to be a treat for Mr Blewitt's birthday.

'Shall I save some of the sprouts for Dad?' asked Robert, hopefully, serving up.

'No, dear,' said Mrs Blewitt. 'I'm afraid he's working late again. I'm not expecting him until half past nine at the earliest. His clients need the figures for the revised development by Thursday.'

Robert peered mournfully into the colander and put another large spoonful of sprouts on everyone's plate.

Sebastian felt distinctly aggrieved.

'Why did this have to happen when I'm home,' he said. 'I hardly ever come home. When I come home it's supposed to be special.'

Eunice threw him a withering look.

'Because your Sacred Texts went and gave the police Fridays off,' she said. 'It's turned into a house-breakers' field day. It's surprising we've still got the tiles on the roof. By next week we probably won't have.'

The sound of the front door opening distracted everyone.

Mr Blewitt managed a brave smile, but he looked tired to death.

'Sprouts,' he said. 'That's nice.'

Mrs Blewitt went to help him with his jacket.

'We weren't expecting you,' she said. 'Did you decide

to finish early, after all?'

Mr Blewitt looked uneasy.

'Not exactly,' he said. 'We had some news.'

'News? What sort of news?'

Mr Blewitt sat down.

'About the casino. They've submitted new plans for the entrance. It's really going to be very grand.'

'Oh dear. And I suppose that means even more intrusive,' said Mrs Blewitt.

'Very intrusive,' said Mr Blewitt, heavily. 'In fact– in fact so intrusive that the shopping centre project has had to be shelved. They might even have to find a completely different site.'

'Oh no,' said Mrs Blewitt. 'Oh dear. And the City did need it. Still, that does mean you won't have to work such long hours, doesn't it? You'll be able to catch up on your model-making. And your jogging.'

Mr Blewitt looked down at the plate of fish fingers and sprouts that Eunice plonked down in front of him and he winced slightly.

'I won't have to work any hours at all,' he said. 'I've been made redundant.'

Chapter 34

It hadn't seemed possible that Eunice would still be quite so spitting mad next morning, but if anything she was even worse.

'But why should *I* suffer just because the sacred divining rods have gone round the twist?' she demanded.

She'd just realized that her typewriter, which she never ever used, had been stolen with the other things in the shed and she seemed to hold Sebastian personally responsible.

'Oh dear, dear,' said Mrs Blewitt, quite shocked. 'I don't like to hear you speaking like that about sacred things.'

'And why not?' demanded Eunice. 'Just what have they ever done for me? I mean, what if I don't like what the sacred things say? What can I do about it?'

There was a pause and then Robert said: 'Move.'

Eunice actually stamped her foot.

'Why should I? It's a dictatorship, that's what it is. We can vote out the Council if they mess things up, but we're stuck with every law having to be approved by some stupid old High Priest and his pathetic apprentice!'

'Oh dear,' said Mrs Blewitt, 'you shouldn't talk so, darling. Especially in front of Sebastian.'

'Anyway, there's nothing wrong with the Sacred Texts,' said Sebastian, doughtily. 'Some of them are quite funny.'

Mrs Blewitt came swiftly to his defence.

'Quite right,' she said. 'The Sacred Texts have been guiding us for thousands of years: and just look how prosperous and contented we've all been.'

'Oh yes, tremendously contented,' sneered Eunice. 'I just love baking, don't I and Robert and Edward adore chasing a bag of air about. And as for the pleasures of Dad's losing his job and half our possessions being stolen and the Holy Hill being dug up for that stupid casino ... do you really expect me to say "Bless His holy name"?'

Mr Blewitt spread some more sprout purée on his toast.

'Young people are bound to have doubts,' he said. 'It's all part of growing up.'

Eunice swung round on him so furiously that for a moment he looked as if he was thinking of diving under the table.

'They aren't doubts,' she announced. 'I'm quite certain about it all. I've just listened to the news and there was another big fight last night and there's been a little boy injured. So I've made up my mind. I'm joining the march on Friday.'

'Oh dear,' said Mrs Blewitt. 'Oh, what a terrible thing. Whatever were his parents thinking of, to let him out? Er ... what march, darling?'

'The *March For Freedom*,' said Eunice, her cheeks

flushed and her head held high. 'To protest about having our laws changed by the Temple.'

Mrs Blewitt blinked at her.

'But ... what about school?' she asked.

'I shan't be going to school!'

'Oh. But what about your exams, darling?'

Eunice marched proudly to the door.

'I'm making the sacrifice in the cause of freedom!' she declared, went out and slammed the door behind her.

'Oh dear,' said Mrs Blewitt, again, when the echoes had died away. 'I don't like to think of Eunice's being involved in something like that.'

'But it's her democratic right,' pointed out Robert.

'Yes, but democratic rights won't help her get into university,' said Edward.

'It's not that,' said Mrs Blewitt, surprisingly. 'I'm afraid there might be trouble.'

'Not with the police,' said Robert. 'Not on a Friday.'

'No,' agreed Mrs Blewitt. 'But there'll be a big crowd and some of them will be excited ... I know we've all rather laughed at Finley Wortle all these years, parading up and down with his sandwich board, but he's got himself quite a following, suddenly. There was an article in *The Warden* about his being the champion of the people and I've heard that Councillor Kimber's men have been seen talking to him. I'm not sure this march is going to be safe.'

'But this is the City,' objected Edward. 'It's famous for being safe.'

'Yes. But I'm very much afraid that things have changed. I mean, it's *not* safe, is it? There was that poor little boy and that old lady who'd only just gone out to water her flowers. Just think, she was probably someone's great-aunt. I can hardly believe how scared people are, suddenly and, I must admit, they've got very good reason.'

Mr Blewitt had been sitting, quiet and thoughtful, stroking his beard. Now he suddenly looked up.

'Eunice will be quite safe,' he said. 'Because I will be on the protest march with her.'

Mrs Blewitt and her sons gazed at him wildly: but Mr Blewitt's mild face was troubled.

'You're quite right, dear,' he said, with unusual certainty. 'Things have changed: everything has gone wrong. Think of it. There are gangs terrorizing the streets and shops are being looted. And I've come to the conclusion that I owe it to the City to do what I can to put it right.'

'I'll come too,' said Mrs Blewitt, suddenly.

'And me!'

'And me!'

Sebastian looked round at his rebellious family and for once he was lost for words. His family–well, his family were useless: they never did anything.

If the Blewitts were taking matters into their own hands, then things were really serious.

Sebastian thought long and hard as he packed his bag to go back to the Temple. He thought about Gerald, breakfasting on plain rat-mix and celery; he thought about the sprouts churning round in his belly; he thought about Mr and Mrs Blewitt and Eunice and Robert and Edward; he thought about Councillor Kimber, planning a revolution; he thought about the High Priest shut up, scared, unhappy and guilty, in his room; and he thought about how very few of the old people dared come to the Temple on a Friday any more.

Mr Meeno needed sorting out, he did. Mr Meeno and his gang.

And Horace, too. Definitely Horace, too.

Sebastian zipped up his bag. He still didn't know what Mr Meeno was planning. Mr Meeno had the casino thing all sorted out already, so this Friday thing must be part of some other plan. But it would be something big– something really magnificent– because Mr Meeno was an exceptionally big and magnificent sort of person.

The traffic on the way back to the Temple was even more snarled-up than usual.

'It's this blessed casino,' said Bert, drumming his fingers

on the steering wheel. 'They're digging up Kurdle Street, now. Must be because of the drains or something, because it's a good way away from the casino site. I reckon they'll have dug half the hill up before they've finished.'

Sebastian opened his window a bit. The pneumatic drills were at work already, tunnelling under the Holy Hill. He'd have to make jolly sure they didn't go anywhere near the Temple. Sebastian thought of the Temple's wide high dome and felt a stab of anxiety. It might not take much to bring the whole thing crashing down. And if it happened when the Temple was full, at Offerings, say–

And then he suddenly knew. He knew why Mr Meeno had arranged for the police to have Fridays off and he knew why Mr Meeno was building a casino on the Holy Hill. He even knew why Mr Meeno had come to the City in the first place.

'Turn left,' he said.

Bert's eyes met Sebastian's in his driving mirror.

'That's a one-way street,' he pointed out.

'I'm in a hurry,' said Sebastian.

Turville produced the plans for the new casino in half an hour. There was a transparent overlay that showed the new entrance.

'It's going to be ever so grand,' admitted Turville. 'All antiqued flagstones and carriage lamps. Quite splendid.

Oh, but it is a pity about the new shopping centre. Poor Councillor Kimber is quite devastated, poor lamb. And I must say I was looking forward to having some shops just round the corner: you've no idea what an effort it can be coming up the hill with a bag full of shopping. And there was me, thinking that if we had a department store just across the square then I'd be able to pop in any old time, even while you were doing lessons.'

Sebastian viewed the plan carefully.

'Turville!'

'Yes, Your Knowingness?'

'What do you know about Mr Meeno?'

The gold pendant that Turville wore round his neck flashed.

'That he's safest left alone, Your Knowingness, I should say.'

Sebastian stroked Gerald's back and Gerald arched himself luxuriously against his hand. Leaving Mr Meeno alone was plainly excellent advice. Except–

'Where does he live, Turville?'

'Oh, he's got a lovely house down by the river. And he's got rooms at his offices in Bullion Street, too.'

Bullion Street. Sebastian traced the name on the map in front of him.

'He'll be looking out at the back of the casino,' he said, thoughtfully.

'That's right, Your Knowingness. It won't be very nice

having one of those noisy things on his doorstep, will it?'

'It might be quite fun,' said Sebastian. 'Or –'

Or Mr Meeno might not be planning to be living there much longer.

'There's a lot of gold in the City, isn't there?' he said, suddenly. 'In big vaults.'

Turville's face suddenly became guarded.

'So they say,' he agreed.

'And ... is it important? I mean,' he went on, hastily, 'I know it's worth a lot of money and all that. But is it important in any other way? What would happen if it was to be – well – stolen? Stolen and taken right away from the City?'

A stray ray of sunlight must have found something to reflect it into the room, for Turville's face glowed, just for a split second, but then it winked out and there was only Turville, fiddling with one of his bracelets.

'The gold is the most important thing in the world,' he said, quietly. 'It's the nest of Ora, bless His holy name: it contains all the love the people have ever had for Him. Haven't you learned about it with Mr Walty, Your Knowingness?'

Sebastian thought back to a story about a young man sinking in the mud and a young woman who gave Ora a stone the colour of honey as a thank-you for saving his life and how Ora had cherished it as a token of her love.

'If the gold were to leave the City – if it all got broken up –'

Turville shook his head decisively.

'That would never happen,' he said. 'Ora would never allow it. The love of the people is precious to Him and always will be and the gold is bound up with it all. All those offerings, over all those years; all those tiny offerings of gold from people who have died and been forgotten, except by Ora, who never forgets and loves everybody still.'

'But – look – say the gold did get taken away and, say, Ora left with it. Just say. Would that make a lot of difference to things?'

Turville gave him an odd look.

'That depends on how important you think Ora is, doesn't it,' he said.

And Sebastian was unable to get any more out of him.

Chapter 35

'You know the gold,' said Sebastian, when Mr Walty arrived for lessons. 'The vaults and all that. Is there anything in the Sacred Texts about them?'

Mr Walty looked surprised.

'Well, yes, of course there is, Blewitt.'

'Oh. Can we do that bit now, then?'

Mr Walty blinked.

'Well ... I suppose we can,' he said, rather disconcerted. 'If you're interested.'

'Yeah,' said Sebastian. 'I am.' And he put his chin in his hands to listen.

It came to pass that Ora was walking in the City when He heard great sounds of wailing and sorrow. And He looked, and there was an infant and her mother, and they both wept, though the infant was making by far the most noise.

And the noise of the infant was so displeasing to Ora–and indeed to all the neighbours, who were all saying 'Oh no, not again!' and slamming their windows shut–that He appeared, but to the infant, only; and the glorious radiance of His countenance was so wondrous that the infant finally shut up its screaming and made noises like water in a drain-pipe, instead.

And then the mother stopped her weeping, too, and gave thanks to Ora, and said: 'At last! The time of sorrow is over, and now perhaps I can get on with the ironing in peace and quietness. And, if I'm lucky, I might even get a chance to read the problem page and grab a nap before the others come home from school. Great is Ora, and bless His holy name for ever, and this is certainly worth an extra bit of gold leaf for the Temple, this is.'

And Ora was warmed by the love of the woman and the infant, and He made a vow, and He said: 'Truly, even though these people are not perfect, still are they part of my being. And though this woman and this infant will bloom and fade and be no more about the streets of the City, yet still will they live in my heart, and the love they bear for me shall shine for ever. And I shall make a safe place in the heart of the City, and in it I shall gather together all the shining love that the people have offered me, and there shall it remain. And I shall warm myself upon it, and it will be dear to me, even as the people are.'

And so it came to pass.

'Yeah,' said Sebastian. 'Yeah. You can see why the gold vaults are so important to Ora, all right. That was a good bit, that was.'

'Humph,' said Mr Walty. 'I suppose so.'

'Well, it was,' said Sebastian. 'What was wrong with it, then?'

Mr Walty shifted in his seat.

'The idea of quietening a squalling child like that,' he said. 'So unlikely. When I think of all the shouting I have to do in school ...'

'Yeah,' said Sebastian, 'but then, people do learn things. Even I learnt things. Sometimes. When you really bawled your head off.'

Mr Walty sighed.

'Actually, I quite enjoy the shouting,' he admitted. 'And I suppose teaching is a worthwhile job. But I'm not sure I can take the stress much longer, Sebastian. The responsibility. The ingratitude. The juvenile body-odour.'

Mr Walty had to come back to the Temple that afternoon for his class's annual Offerings visit. Sebastian put on the full disco-lights and laser show, together with the underwater conjuror and the performing skunks.

Sebastian kept a very careful eye on Horace Meeno and so, fortunately, did Mrs Poash. She discovered him fiddling with Sebastian's aqualung, scolded him thoroughly and made him sit next to her until home time.

Sebastian made a point of thanking her.

'It's no trouble,' she said, quite graciously. 'Horace reminds me a little of my own son and so I always recognize him. He's a nice little boy, really, for all his mischief.'

'What, Horace?'

'Well, he's an orphan, you know, poor mite,' said Mrs Poash, vaguely. 'And he seems strangely drawn to the Temple. I quite often see him here. I tell myself that Ora must have sent him for a reason.'

Sebastian shook his head.

'It's not like that,' he said. 'Ora doesn't send people places. He lets us all do as we please. You see, it's because He likes us.'

'Well,' said Mrs Poash. 'I think Horace's challenging behaviour may be a cry for help.'

'Huh,' said Sebastian.

Turville was very quiet the next morning.

'You got a cold?' asked Sebastian. 'You keep sniffing.'

'Oh no, Your Knowingness. No, I never get ill. It's just that everyone is so angry and so afraid and thinking such ugly thoughts.'

'Yeah,' said Sebastian. 'Well, that's life, isn't it.'

Turville gave a deep shudder.

'It is,' he said. 'Oh, it is. And I can't help wondering if life was all a terrible mistake. The Blue Plague was a terrible time–there have been many, many terrible times – but people have always had Ora to turn to, for comfort. But now people are losing their faith in Ora. They're losing their need for Him, I think. Sometimes all life seems to have brought us is a lot of ugliness and pain. Perhaps the universe would be better off without life.'

'Nah,' said Sebastian. 'I like it. And anyway, if there wasn't any life, Ora would be lonely, wouldn't He?'

And at that Turville laughed until he cried.

Chapter 36

Getting rid of Mr Meeno was a huge project, but Sebastian didn't have time for huge projects. He had Offerings every afternoon and usually at least an hour's eating cakes with Mr Walty in the mornings and that usually only left Sebastian two or three free hours at a stretch.

What Sebastian needed was a day off. Tomorrow would be ideal, because it was a Friday, so Mr Meeno would be working on his master plan: that meant that Sebastian could investigate without having to worry about the police.

'I mean, *everybody* gets days off, don't they?' Sebastian said to Mr Walty. 'It's only right that people should have days off. I mean, you can't expect people to go on and on and on, can you? Not without having a single day's rest.'

'But you have Saturdays and Sundays off,' pointed out Mr Walty, brushing crumbs off his woolly paunch.

'I still have to do Offerings,' said Sebastian, doggedly. 'I've done Offerings every day since I've got here. I know the High Priest's really busy with his praying and all that – and that he's not feeling so great – and no one would expect him to do the tap-dancing or the cartwheels or the abseiling – but a day off! I reckon that'd give me a whole new lease of life.'

'Really?' said Mr Walty, blenching.

Sebastian scowled at the table.

'The puppet show and the jazz combo can manage by themselves, really,' he said. 'I mean, the High Priest doesn't have to do the bit where the drummer throws me his drumsticks and I do a drum roll on the Bowl of Offering. Or the bit where one of the puppets has a gold coin on the end of a kite, and I bounce up on the trampoline to get it. I mean, that's all optional, isn't it?'

'Yes, yes,' said Mr Walty. 'Well. Well, I don't see why you shouldn't have the occasional day off, especially if it was on a Friday. Mrs Walty hasn't been happy about my coming out on Fridays ever since someone put the car up on the garage roof.'

'Cor! Really? Did you get it down again?'

'Oh, yes, that was no bother. The annoying thing was that Number 25's rabbit was shut up in it and it'd nibbled holes in the upholstery. We're having ever such a lot of bother with the insurance.'

Sebastian talked to Turville after lessons.

'I do *like* serving in the Temple and all that,' said Sebastian. 'Of course I do. Even though I keep having strange accidents; like yesterday, when I nearly sat on that poisonous thorn somebody had left on my throne. Cor, but it's a good job Mrs Poash was keeping an eye out. No, of course I like Offerings. But I don't want to get all worn out and miserable, like the High Priest, do

I? I mean, sometimes it does you good to have a break, doesn't it?'

'It can do,' said Turville, neutrally. 'What sort of break were you thinking of having, Your Knowingness?'

Sebastian shrugged.

'I thought I'd just wander about a bit.'

'You'll get mobbed, Your Knowingness. You'll have everybody swarming round wanting autographs.'

'Not if I wore ordinary clothes, they wouldn't.'

But Turville was still doubtful.

'I wouldn't worry so much if it wasn't a Friday,' he said. 'But you know what Fridays are like.'

'No,' said Sebastian, promptly. 'I don't. I spend all my Fridays cooped up in here. Every day's the same to me.'

'And there's going to be a protest march,' said Turville. 'Just think of it, a protest march in the City. And no police about, either. Just Finley and a crowd of supporters and perhaps some of Councillor Kimber's men in with them.'

'Yeah. Well, it'll be really interesting to see something like that,' said Sebastian. 'And I ought to know what people are doing, oughtn't I?'

Turville's face sharpened.

'You aren't thinking of joining the protest march, are you?' he asked. 'Because in your position–'

'Oh no,' said Sebastian, with the most transparent sincerity. 'Oh no. I definitely wouldn't do a thing like that. I mean, what would happen if I was recognized?'

'Hm.'

Turville flicked a bright duster over the table top, but there was a moodiness to his wrist-action that suggested an unquiet mind.

'The shops will be closed,' he said.

'That's all right, I don't like shopping. It's just that Friday is the best day for Mr Walty, on account of Mrs Walty's being worried about rabbits eating the car.'

'And what about Offerings?'

'The High Priest can do it just this once.'

Turville sighed.

'I suppose if I tell him you've got the day off he'll do his best,' he said. 'He can't feel bad about breaking off his prayers for Offerings, can he? And if I look out his bullet-proof vest ...'

'His what?'

Turville looked vague.

'He's very sensitive,' he said. Then he suddenly put down the duster and faced Sebastian squarely.

'Now look,' he said. 'I know it's not my place, Your Knowingness, but I can't help but worry.'

'But I only want a bit of a wander round,' said Sebastian, allowing himself to sound a little plaintive. 'Boys do that sort of thing, don't they? Just a little mooch around the houses. After all, Ora will look after me.'

'You know it doesn't work like that,' said Turville, warningly. 'What about all those people who have been found in the river? Ora didn't save them, did He? What about Mrs Poash's boy who died of a fever when he was no bigger than you?'

That was a real shock.

'Oh. I didn't know he was dead,' said Sebastian. 'Oh. I see. So that's why she thinks Ora's out to get her, then.'

'Yes. That's why.'

'But still,' went on Sebastian. 'It might be a bit dangerous and all that out in the City, but I don't mind that too much. I've always done stuff other people don't do. And, I mean, Ora must quite like me, mustn't He? I must have been chosen for a reason, mustn't I? I mean, He must like having me around.'

Turville suddenly smiled.

'Of course He does,' he said. 'Well, just take care, then.'

And he advanced no further argument.

'The first thing I have to do is to find the vaults,' said Sebastian. 'I already know they'll be somewhere around the casino building site.'

Gerald sniffed intelligently at the map.

'And then,' went on Sebastian, 'and then–and then I'll make Mr Meeno go away and then everything will be all right again.'

Gerald didn't have the facilities for raising an eyebrow, but his expression could hardly have been more sceptical if he had.

'Well, I can spy around a bit, can't I?' said Sebastian. 'And if I find anything suspicious – a heap of gold dust or something – then I can sneak off very quietly and I can tell the police first thing on Saturday. Can't I? I can start at the Bullion Street offices. I'll dress up as a meter-reader and –'

Gerald heaved a small but withering sigh and Sebastian thought about it more carefully.

'All right,' he conceded, 'I'll go as ... as someone else. I'll go as someone wanting a job. Not a grown-up job, all right, but something like ... er ... cleaning cars, or ... or ... keeping a lookout. Yeah, I'd be a really good lookout, wouldn't I, because no one would ever suspect me of being part of a hardened criminal gang. I could just sort of lounge on a street corner, playing with a yo-yo, say and no one would realize that my innocent exterior actually masks a cunning criminal mind and a lightning brain of immense power.'

From the way Gerald sniffed, he seemed to agree.

Chapter 37

Sebastian woke up so early on Friday morning that he had time to climb the narrow secret stairs right up to where the sun made the blue and gold glass in the dome hum with warmth. The Temple looked like a forest from up here, all fluted columns and overarching details, motionless and imperishable and whole.

There was just one patch of cold silver staining the honeycomb tiles below him. Sebastian waited until Mrs Poash had finished. Then he went down to meet her.

'All right?'

'Very well, thank you,' she said, with a sniff that would have seemed disapproving if he hadn't seen her tears.

'Nice morning,' said Sebastian.

'Very pleasant indeed.'

Sebastian paused for a moment.

'Yeah,' he said. 'Well, that's because Ora designed it, didn't He? I mean, the Temple, and diseases and stuff, that's nothing much to do with Ora, is it? That's just life. But the morning, that's straight from Him. That's why there's one every single day and it never goes wrong. See?'

Turville made him a packed lunch. Sebastian took some

of the sandwiches, but left the joint of beef and the bowl of salad in the fridge for teatime.

It was odd wearing trousers: it wasn't until he remembered he could plunge his hands into his pockets that he felt at all comfortable. He went out of the back door, mooched round the corner of the Temple and through the broad striped shadows of the portico: and for the first time for ages, Finley Wortle wasn't there.

Sebastian looked back when he had crossed the square. The golden stone of the Temple absorbed the sharp edge of the sunshine and reflected back an embracing warmth. He turned and dived into the maze of alleys and footpaths that dodged between the buildings around Bullion Street.

There weren't many people about and those people he saw kept their faces turned away. Sebastian hadn't been for a walk round the City for a long time, but he didn't remember people doing that. They used to laugh and talk to one another. They used to say 'Morning!' They used to dawdle and look in shop windows. The children used to play football in unsuitable places and call out silly things.

The children would be at school, of course, but there was still something about the City that had changed; even the tourists looked uneasy, almost afraid.

Coo, Mr Meeno wasn't half asking for it, he was.

Bullion Street was a cobbled passage, really. Sebastian went along looking at the dusty and faded doors. And there – yes, there it was: a shining plaque declaring MEENO ASSOCIATES in refined gold letters.

Sebastian pushed firmly at the door.

Locked.

No bell.

Well, he'd have to look for the back door, then. The old part of the City was a maze. Tourists came in two types: there was the sort that spent their whole visit with their noses in a map, failing to see any of the City; and those that got lost immediately and wandered about in a happy daze. Sebastian's search wasn't made easier by the building work that was going on all over the place. Several alleys were blocked by red and white striped tape, or heaps of rubble, or bulldozers, or notices telling everybody to wear a hard hat, but Sebastian managed, by climbing through the cabin of a crane and ignoring several severe notices, to find an alley that contained fifteen bin bags, a white and ginger cat and a small grimy door below an identically crazy arrangement of chimneys to those above Mr Meeno's Bullion Street entrance.

That door was locked, too, but there was a bell-pull handle set into the brickwork and Sebastian had always wanted to work one of those.

It jingled tinnily, a long way away. If no one answered, the easiest thing would be to put a brick through a window. Sebastian hadn't broken a window for ages and there were loads of bits of brick about.

He was scouting around for the absolutely perfect bit of brick when from inside the house there came the sound of bolts being drawn.

Chapter 38

Sebastian hastily dropped his bit of brick and put on a winning smile.

'Hello,' he said, to the young woman who stood champing gum in the doorway. 'Is this where Mr Meeno lives?'

'Who's asking?'

Her off-white hair was crimped into highly symmetrical waves and her voice could have skewered a rhino.

'Jim Walty,' said Sebastian, happily. He thought that inspired. Why, it might liven Mr Walty's life up for him and Mr Walty's life clearly needed enlivening.

The girl switched her gum over to the other cheek and chewed vacantly for a while. Now Sebastian came to think about it, he'd seen her before: yes, that was right, in the Temple, that time, with Mr Meeno.

'So what do you want?' she asked, at last.

'I've come about a job,' said Sebastian.

The girl's face couldn't be said to focus entirely, but something stirred. She opened the door a little wider and Sebastian saw that her clothes must be even more difficult to breathe in than he'd thought.

'I guess you'd better come in,' she said.

Sebastian followed her into a grubby corridor that smelt of disinfectant and cigarettes and then into a room containing a shabby desk, a hatstand, a waste-paper basket and some spotty lino. The young woman wiggled her skirt up a little so she could perch on the desk and she gazed at him through dopey blue eyes.

'Everyone's out,' she said.

'That's all right,' said Sebastian. 'I don't mind waiting.'

He tipped the contents of the bin out tidily into a corner, upturned it and sat himself down comfortably. The girl got a thing like a lolly stick out of a little bag and began to scrape listlessly at one of her maroon nails.

'Nice place,' said Sebastian.

She sniffed.

'You think so?'

'Yeah. Yeah, I do. Must be boring for you, though, being stuck in here by yourself.'

She sighed, dramatically.

'You're telling me. A sophisticated lady like what I am is used to a more sociable lifestyle.'

Sebastian nodded, wondered vaguely what she was talking about and wished he'd brought Gerald along, as a conversation piece.

'I've got a rat at home,' he said, trying it anyway.

'A wild rat.'

That actually caught her interest. You could tell by the way her eyes swivelled and her gum-chewing accelerated.

'Now, don't you talk to me about rats,' she said, in a voice that could strip paint at twenty paces. 'This whole place is swarming with them. I tells Mr Meeno, I says, "Put poison down." But would he? No. "We got to abide by the rules of the City," that's what Mr Meeno said. So I says "Meeno," I says, "I'll stick to you through thick and thin, but I ain't living in no rat-infested house." That's what I tell him, straight. But would he do anything about it? Not one thing.'

'He sounds a really kind man,' said Sebastian, sincerely.

The girl shook her primrose hair a little and then patted it down again.

'I guess he ain't so bad. He had them stop up all the holes in my room, but you can still hear them scurrying about. Ugh!' She broke off with a shudder. 'Still, we won't be here much longer. "Honey," Meeno says to me the other night, "when I've finished my business in this god-awful dump I'll take you somewhere nice and warm, and I'm going to buy you a diamond ring and a mink coat." Well, I says to him, "Meeno," I says, "if you take me somewhere warm then I won't need a mink coat!" He likes that. He really likes it when I'm smart.'

'So ... you're leaving soon, then,' said Sebastian, elaborately casual, though his heart was beating fast.

She shrugged.

'So they say. I just wish I knew when, that's all. Mr Meeno, he don't never tell me nothing at all. "Meeno," I says, "I won't tell no one!" and he says, "Not if you don't know nothing to tell, sweetheart." And he just thinks he's so smart. Still, there's men for you. And then he goes off and leaves me in this rat-infested hovel for hours and hours at a time, with no one to talk to. It wouldn't be so bad if the shops was open. But what's a girl to do with herself, that's what I want to know.'

Sebastian tapped himself on the chest.

'Ah,' he said, 'well, today's your lucky day.'

Honey raised a discontented arch of paint over a baby-blue eye.

'Hadn't noticed it, so far.'

'No,' said Sebastian, patiently, 'but that was because I hadn't got here. No wonder you were fed up when anyone can see you're one of those people who should be out and about enjoying themselves. I mean, it's a waste, your being stuck in this dusty old place where no one can enjoy your company.'

Honey wriggled a little.

'So how come it's my lucky day?' she asked.

Sebastian beamed.

'Because I,' he said, with pride and absolute assurance, 'am a fully-qualified rat-charmer!'

Chapter 39

The house rambled along beside the alley a little way and then over to Bullion Street. It must originally have been several different buildings, because there were quite a few places where the floors weren't quite on the same level and lots of unexpected turnings in the corridors and bits of fancy ceiling that ran out in the middle of walls.

'Yes,' said Sebastian, peering into a chilly room that contained a grimy bed and a heap of unclean clothes. 'I see.'

'That's Harry's room,' said Honey, through a new piece of gum. The last piece she'd spat politely out of the window. 'Disgusting, ain't it. And he expects me to pick up after him. "Harry," I says, "I ain't no servant, so just you remember it." That shuts him up, especially when Meeno hears about it. "I ain't having no lady friend treated like no servant." That's what he says.'

'Mm,' said Sebastian, tapping a wall. 'I don't think this is it. No. Sorry. We'll have to look a bit further.'

Honey gave a ladylike shiver.

'Well, I can't say I'm surprised,' she said. 'If I was prime minister of the rats I wouldn't want to hold my parliament here. Shall I show you the rest of the house?'

Sebastian heaved a sigh.

'I'm afraid you're going to have to,' he said. 'I mean, the attics are usually the place, but in this house it must be somewhere else. You must have a room somewhere that's especially attractive to them.'

A resigned expression passed over Honey's face, like the heaving of an over-loaded washing machine.

'Well, they certainly like my room,' she said. 'But all the rat holes is blocked up, like I tell you. Shall I show you anyway?'

Honey opened a door on what was easily the most repulsive room that Sebastian had ever set eyes on. It was pink and it was flounced and it was frilly.

'Er ... no,' said Sebastian, his nose twitching at the onslaught of a dozen clashing perfumes. 'This wouldn't suit a rat at all.'

Honey smirked.

'Refined, ain't it,' she said, complacently. 'Guess it's too ladylike for them. Come on, I'll show you the rest.'

'Now this here is Horace's room,' she announced. 'He's Mr Meeno's nephew.'

Sebastian peered through the doorway. The window looked out at a brick wall, and, except for a narrow bed and a lot of pictures of film-star baddies that had been torn from magazines there was very little in there.

'He hasn't even got a telly,' said Sebastian, amazed:

he'd assumed Horace would have everything at least twice over.

Honey shrugged.

'Mr Meeno's a busy man,' she said. 'Anyhow, even a rat wouldn't fancy sharing with Horace. I'll show you downstairs.'

There were several rooms there containing leather furniture and complicated rugs. Sebastian had looked into a dining room and a television room before Honey paused outside the next door.

'I'm not sure about showing you in here,' she said. 'I'm not sure Mr Meeno would like it.'

'No? Why not?'

'It's his business room. He's kinda fussy about people going in. You know how it is with business people.'

Sebastian nodded solemnly. 'Well, I don't suppose it'll be this one, anyway,' he said. 'I'll just test it, to make sure.'

He took off his deep-sea diving watch and set it to show fathoms.

'Can I borrow your chewing gum for a minute, Miss Honey?'

'Why, sure, if it helps.' She hoicked it out elegantly and presented it to him on a finger. Sebastian used it to stick the watch to the door.

'Just have to wait a few moments for the reading to settle,' he explained.

'Gee!'

Honey peered at the watch through her periwinkle eyes. If she could have understood the reading, it told her she was not under water.

'There!' said Sebastian, after an impressive pause. 'Look at that. Zero!'

Honey blinked twiggy eyelashes at the little dial. 'Gracious! Does that mean the prime minister rat's in there?'

'Practically certain, with those readings. Hardly ever seen an all-the-zeroes before. Oh yes. Yes. You get a nose for it, in the rat business.'

'Truly, Mr Walty?'

'Yeah. Er ... it goes sort of tingly inside the nostrils.'

'And is it tingling now?'

'Yeah. It's coming at me right through the door, really strong. Look,' he went on, 'I don't like to think of a nice lady like you having to put up with all those rats. So I'll tell you what I'll do. You just leave me in there for half an hour or so and I'll see what I can do to charm up the prime minister rat. Then, once I've charmed him, I'll make him go right away and take all his quangos with him. And then you can rest easy. OK?'

'Gee!' said Honey. 'I'd sure like that. It sure does make a girl uneasy to lie in bed at night wondering if she's going to have hairy vermin crawling all over her. But I don't quite know if Mr Meeno would like it.'

'That's OK,' said Sebastian. 'Seeing as you're such a nice lady and that you're in such trouble, I'll do it for free. Then Mr Meeno won't ever have to know. How about that?'

Mr Meeno's study had a massive desk and a whole wall of bookcases. Sebastian ran his eyes over the room, but he couldn't see anything out of the ordinary.

'How do you charm 'em?' asked Honey, behind him.

He turned round hastily.

'Oh, that's a family secret,' he said. 'It's been passed down from uncle to nephew for centuries, it has. The secret is whispered to you on the evening of your tenth birthday and if you tell anyone then you get struck down by the family curse and your ears fall off.'

'Fancy!' said Honey.

'I have to do a special sort of whistling and that attracts them.'

'Gee. And how do you know which one is the prime minister rat?'

Sebastian took a long deep breath to give himself time to work that one out.

'It's the glitter in its eyes,' he said at last. 'Sort of mean and vicious.'

Honey let out a squeak of horror.

'But just as long as you stay outside the door and keep it tight shut you'll be all right,' said Sebastian, reassuringly. 'I won't let it get at you, don't you worry.'

The moment Honey shut the door Sebastian moved. None of the silver-bound decanters operated a secret trapdoor and none of them contained anything that smelt drinkable. Only one drawer of the desk wasn't empty and that only contained circulars about weight-reducing tablets and a largely empty appointments diary. Sebastian ducked under the desk to check for secret levers.

'Hey!'

Sebastian jumped so violently he bashed his head.

'Hey, how's it going?'

Only Honey. And she was still outside the door. Sebastian stuck out his tongue in a pant of relief.

'Haven't got 'em out, yet,' he called. 'The prime minister's really tough, this one is.'

'Oh. Because I can't hear no whistling or nothing.'

Blow: he hadn't thought of that.

'Ah. Well, that's interesting, that is.'

'No, really?'

'Oh, yes ... er ... rats, they can hear sounds so high that people can't hear them at all.'

'Is that so?'

'Yeah. And my special rat charming, well, only rats can hear it. That's why we're all young, you see, us rat-charmers: once our voices break, we just can't do the charming any more. Tragic, it is, to know that all my talents are going to vanish in just a few years.'

'Well,' came Honey's voice, through the wood of the door. 'Who would have thought that a common or garden rat would be so clever?'

'Amazing, isn't it,' agreed Sebastian. 'But just give me half an hour and I should have them all sorted, just you wait and see.' And to his relief Honey's spiky little heels tapped away down the corridor.

This was a truly horrible room: it made him feel prickly, as if it were full of invisible eyes. He looked round sharply, but the painting of the dark-eyed man was, as far as he could see, only that. But it was still sending shivers up and down his spine.

Sebastian took a grip on himself. The Temple was a thousand times more awe-inspiring than this place and that gave him no trouble at all. It was crazy to get the jitters here. Sebastian carried on his search. In fact he found he felt fine when he was walking about. It was only when he stood still that he found himself quivering.

It was worst of all on the polished parquet floor, he discovered and once he'd realized that, he twigged what was going on. He squatted down and felt the floor with the palm of his hand. Yes, there was no doubt about it: faintly, but definitely, the floor was trembling. From time to time there were tiny shocks among the vibrations:

sometimes singly, sometimes in two or three second bursts. It might be being caused by the demolition work outside, except that somehow it was too regular, too gentle, too planned. This was something being made, he was sure, not something being destroyed.

But what?

Sebastian drew in a deep breath to control the shoots of excitement that were sprouting up inside him. A tunnel. That was what it would have to be. Someone was building a tunnel deep down in the golden heart of the City and it probably started from somewhere near here.

He began to search again, quicker. He looked at every piece of paper he could find. He lifted every picture on the wall: but neither the murky brown marshes nor the boisterous scarf-waving ladies had anything behind them but dust and web-wrapped shards of moth.

He stopped and scowled round. Didn't Mr Meeno and his gang watch spy movies? He'd spent fifteen minutes in here and he'd searched all the places that should have hidden the secret lever that opened the tunnel entrance.

He needed to find something out of place; something that didn't quite belong ...

And then, in a curlicued mirror, he saw it.

Of course. He'd been looking for something small, something hidden, but this was so big that he'd disregarded it. It was so big it took up a whole wall.

Books. Sets and sets of them, in neat tooled leather, golden names gleaming discreetly. Mr Meeno was no doubt exceedingly bright, but whether Mr Meeno ever sat down and perused these sorts of books was quite another thing. They didn't look like the sort of books that *anyone* would want to read, not even earnest and boring people like Edward.

In fact, when Sebastian looked closely, the gold leaf on the top edges of the pages was coated with a muting layer of dust.

Sebastian pulled over a heavy chair and stood up on it. He found what he was looking for almost straight away. As he squinted along the rows of books, a gleam of extra brightness caught his eye. Yes, there it was. Someone had disturbed the dust on volume fifteen of *The History of The Marshes*.

The book had a perfectly ordinary dull green spine with tiny gold letters on it. But ...

Sebastian jumped down from the chair and pulled at it, as if he were taking it off the shelf.

There was a sweet *chunk*, as if of the most well-oiled and expensive machinery and the whole bookshelf swung open, just like it did in the movies. It knocked the chair sideways with a graunch of wood on wood.

Sebastian peered into the deep recesses that revealed themselves behind it. There was a safe, set into the wall and there – Sebastian gulped – there was a man.

He was squinting up at Sebastian from under the rim of his hat.

And he had a sentry guard look about him that made Sebastian quite sure that Mr Meeno wasn't far away.

Chapter 40

'Hey,' said the man. 'What the –'

'Hi,' said Sebastian, rallying, as brightly as he could. 'You must work for Mr Meeno, right?'

The man scowled and took a blackjack out of his inside pocket. Sebastian couldn't help noticing how terribly at ease that man was with that blackjack; he looked as if he'd been wielding blackjacks since he was a boy and that was obviously many years before.

'Yeah,' said the man, who was a dead lookalike of a badly shaved orang-utan, but without the charm.

'I'm Jim Walty,' said Sebastian, promptly. 'I've come about the rats.'

The man looked confused, as if someone had sneaked up and pinched his bunch of bananas. Perhaps if Sebastian could just confuse him a bit more, then maybe –

Another head came out of the darkness. It had sleek dark hair and bright black eyes and it looked as though it had never been confused in its life. It twitched a cigar from one side of its mouth to the other and rapped out:

'Who's this guy?'

'Name of Walty, boss. Come about the rats.'

Sebastian smiled bravely, even though the lump of cold metal that had suddenly formed in his stomach was telling him he was doomed.

'The lady said you've been having trouble with them,' he explained. 'So I'm ... er ... I'm just charming them out.'

Mr Meeno came up out of the darkness with an energy and briskness that didn't go with his advanced age. Sebastian's eyes were adjusting now and behind Mr Meeno he could make out a ladder and the beginning of a tunnel nearly big enough to walk through.

'What kind of a place is this?' demanded Mr Meeno. 'High Priests and Temples and Councils, yeah, I can handle them – but a rat – charmer? Tell me I'm dreaming, Jerome.'

'You're dreaming, boss,' said Jerome, promptly.

Mr Meeno rolled his eyes to heaven.

'What I miss,' he said, to the world at large, 'is intellectual companionship. I mean, what's a guy like me to do when he's surrounded by chicken-brains, huh? I mean, I ask ya!'

Mr Meeno looked Sebastian up and down. Sebastian kept an ingratiating smile carefully glued to his face, but Mr Meeno showed no sign of warming to it.

'Jerome!' he snapped.

'Yes, boss?'

'I'm not sure I like this Walty guy, Jerome.'

A spark of interest flickered in Jerome's murky eyes.

'Shall I hit him, boss?' he asked, hopefully.

Mr Meeno paused, as if for consideration.

'Well, it'd get rid of him sure enough,' he conceded. 'But do we really want a body on our hands at this particular juncture?'

'I could dump him in the river,' Jerome offered.

Sebastian had been right: he *was* doomed.

Mr Meeno took his fat cigar from between his teeth, inspected the tip narrowly and put it back again.

'Nah,' he said. 'Not now. Put him on ice until I can give the matter my careful consideration.'

'OK, boss,' said Jerome.

Sebastian didn't argue with the blackjack. It was small, that blackjack, but it had presence, like a scorpion.

Jerome tied him to a chair. Jerome was not bright, but he was good at tying people up: there was absolutely no point in struggling.

It wasn't long before several more men emerged from the tunnel. They all looked tired and none of them looked happy, but when Mr Meeno asked if everything was OK, they said 'Sure, boss.'

'So when are we set to go?' asked the boss.

'Any time you say, boss,' said Slats, who still hadn't

succeeded in swallowing his golf ball. 'The fuses is all laid snug and ready. You say the word and – *ka boom!*'

Mr Meeno walked up and down rubbing his hands together.

'Well,' he said, 'I've never found there to be any gain in dawdling. It's noon now, so that gives us a clear twelve hours before the cops clock in for duty. So we go this afternoon, OK? Five thirty, when everyone's more fascinated about getting home to their loved ones than enquiring into any explosions that might knock a little dust off their eyebrows.'

There was a certain amount of nodding and satisfied gum-champing among his companions.

'Right,' said Mr Meeno, briskly. 'We clear everything out of here, OK? Harry, get the trucks brought round, I want everything that's worth taking loaded up. The desk and all the *objets d'art*. Got that?'

Harry regarded the desk. It was solid and shiny, and it gave every impression of being extraordinarily heavy.

'But you'll be able to buy yourself the best desk in the whole world, boss,' he pointed out. 'So why shift this one?'

'I dunno,' said Mr Meeno. 'Sentiment, I guess: a lot of intellectual activity went on at that desk. Oh, and Harry!'

'Yes, boss?'

Mr Meeno threw him a bunch of keys.

'Clear out the safe.'

Sebastian sat and watched them work. Four of the men staggered out with the desk and a little while later they came back, rather dishevelled and began to wrap bronze Cavaliers and plaster busts in newspaper. Harry was taking piles of papers out of the safe and packing them tenderly into a cello case. Sebastian smiled to himself. Mr Meeno thought big. He liked that.

Honey came along a little later. Her eyes opened wide when she saw Sebastian.

'Why,' she said, 'Mr Walty! Whatever are you doing all tied up like that?'

Sebastian sighed.

'It's what Mr Meeno wanted,' he said.

'Gee! Why?'

Sebastian shrugged as well as his bonds permitted.

'He didn't say.'

Honey rolled her large blue eyes up to the ceiling.

'Why, ain't that just typical?' she asked. 'It's just the same with me. Now, I am Mr Meeno's *best friend* and he never explains anything to me. You'd think a guy would trust his best friend, wouldn't you? Especially when his best friend's a lady.'

'I expect Mr Meeno just wants to keep you safe,' said Sebastian, with some envy. 'When an important man like

Mr Meeno does business – well, he's bound to have secrets.'

'Oh, he does,' said Honey, pursing up cushiony lips to blow dust delicately off a photograph. 'I know he has to be just so careful.'

'Well, I expect he wants to make sure that no one hurts you,' said Sebastian, with a sigh.

Honey pushed up her hair into even rounder waves.

'I just guess you're right,' she said. 'I bet he wouldn't let no one hurt one little old hair on my little old head. That's what love does to a man.'

Sebastian kept his teeth gritted and managed not to throw up quite easily. Harry had got to the bottom of the safe, now. He felt carefully around inside it, grunted his satisfaction and flicked the catches of the cello case shut. Slats wandered back into the room, re-settling his jacket on his bony shoulders.

'Hey,' said Slats, through his golf ball, 'I'm parched. How about a little refreshment, sweetheart?'

'Yeah,' said the man who followed him in. 'You know, we ain't accustomed to this manual work. You wouldn't want us to faint from exhaustion, now, would you?'

'That'd be the day,' said Honey, disdainfully. 'You lot is more likely to keel over through lack of use. OK, OK, I'll see if I can find something. Don't go away.'

Sebastian heaved a sigh. There he was, tied hand and

foot, surrounded by large and vicious gangsters with a reputation for concrete cobbling and she said 'Don't go away.' And Sebastian suddenly realized really properly that there weren't any circumstances in which this bunch of thugs were going to untie him until it was time to dump him in the river.

Unless –

Chapter 41

'Er ... excuse me, Miss Honey!'

Honey turned in the doorway.

'I'm very sorry to trouble you, Miss Honey, but I'm ever so thirsty, too,' said Sebastian, assuming his most humble and virtuous expression. 'Would it be too much bother for me to have a glass of water, please?'

Slats turned to him with a scowl.

'You shut your mouth!' he snarled, but Honey swiped him pettishly.

'You just leave him alone,' she said. 'He only wants a glass of water and at least he asked nice. I only wish the rest of you was so easily satisfied.'

It wasn't long before the tacking of her little heels heralded her return.

'Well, untie his arms, you great baboon.'

Sebastian flexed his shoulders and rubbed enough feeling back into his wrists to pick up his glass. Being tied up was a lot less fun than he'd thought: bits of you itched and there was nothing you could do about it.

'My,' said Honey, admiringly. 'You *were* thirsty, weren't you, Mr Walty?'

'Saved my life,' said Sebastian. 'Is there any more in the jug?'

'Sure,' said Honey.

Sebastian sat quietly for a few minutes while the men sipped dourly at their drinks and then he began to fidget a bit.

'Er ... excuse me!'

'You shut up!' snarled Harry.

'I'm afraid I need to be untied,' said Sebastian, apologetically.

'Well, ain't that tough.'

'I'm afraid it's urgent,' said Sebastian and Harry cursed.

'Can't you wait?'

Sebastian looked thoughtful.

'I can try,' he said, doubtfully. 'But sometimes there's just no stopping me.'

Harry turned on Honey.

'Did you have to fill him up to the brim?'

'Well, you wouldn't want him dying of thirst, would you?' she retorted. 'You know what Meeno always says about having people die in your own home.'

'He was never going to have time to die of thirst!'

'I don't mind,' put in Sebastian, pathetically, 'but I don't want to spoil the chair.'

Harry cursed some more. 'Well, really,' said Honey. 'You shouldn't use words like that in front of persons of refined sentiment like what Mr Walty and I is. You'll offend our delicate ears.' Harry then bent down to tug at the straps that bound Sebastian's ankles.

'OK,' he growled. 'Out the door. And you make one wrong move and your ears will have more to worry about than language. You got me?'

Sebastian took his time. The bathroom had a small brass statue of Ora on the window sill and a sash window that overlooked the deserted demolition site.

'Hurry up!' snarled Harry, behind him. 'Do you think I've got time to hang about round here while you enjoy the view?'

When they got back to Mr Meeno's study, Honey was perched on the window sill again and the whole room was empty except for the faint scent of aged dust.

'They took the chair,' she announced. 'Guess they don't want to break up the set. I says to them, "It's wanted," I says, but no one round here ever takes any notice. You all treat me as if I'd been born just some dumb blonde or something.'

Harry gave a jagged laugh.

'Come off it,' he said. 'No one would ever accuse *you* of being born blonde.'

The other men had all gone off somewhere, presumably to load the lorry. If Sebastian was going to get out of this alive, then this was going to be as good a chance as he was going to get. But the door was behind him.

Sebastian took a very small step sideways. Harry was

too busy sparring with Honey to notice.

'That's no way to address a lady!' Honey was saying, her voice shrill enough to take the core out of an apple.

'Oh yeah? And what's that got to do with anything?'

Sebastian, very conscious of every pain cell in his body, took another step.

He had never really thought very much about ears, beyond noting that Edward's were large and monkey-like and that Robert's went bright pink when the sun shone through them at breakfast, but he discovered that he was very fond of his ears. They were so sensitive they could detect every draught and tiny variation in temperature: and the thought of what Harry might do to them made it hard to breathe.

'Because I'll tell Meeno, you great heap of horse-meat and then he'll give you the scameroo. That's what.'

Harry smirked.

'I don't think so.'

Sebastian was slightly behind Harry, now and only four steps from the door. Four steps: that was two too many. Sebastian would be within grabbing range all the way and Harry wasn't the man to hesitate. It was unlikely that Harry had done many good deeds in his life, but the reason for that certainly wasn't idleness.

'You don't think so, huh?'

'That's right. And I'll tell you why. Smart, reliable

guys – such as me – is not so easy to come by.'

Honey let out a laugh that could have scoured a saucepan.

'And who says you're smart? Your cousin the gorilla?'

Sebastian took one more very quiet step towards the door. Harry's lips had thinned to cheese-parings.

'Go easy on the wise-talk,' he snarled. 'I hate to see a doll straining herself.'

Honey shook her curls scornfully.

'It's not me who's straining, Harry. You may think you're Meeno's right-hand man, but you know what? You're just the hired help.'

Harry took a step towards her.

'Is that so?'

'Well, yes it is.'

'It is, is it? Then how come it's me who knows what's going on, huh? Who knows what this is all about?'

One more very small step. Mustn't rush it.

Honey waggled her powdered shoulders and pouted her shiny lips.

'That's because Meeno wants for it to be a wonderful surprise,' she said. 'He has to tell you because you're here to do all the work and such. He keeps it from me because he does not want to sully my ladylike purity.'

Harry let out a bark of laughter.

'Yeah and Meeno's a great kidder. There ain't nothing

so special about you. Meeno and me, we go right back. I shared my first cell with him. You know what? You're just another broad.'

Sebastian didn't know much about all that lady stuff, but he thought that a real lady probably wouldn't have even tried to hit Harry – at least, not with the spiky heel of her shoe – and that, if she had, she wouldn't have made half so effective a job of it. Harry's foot slipped as he ducked: and his head hit the wall.

Chapter 42

Sebastian moved. He flung himself through the door, spent a valuable half second slamming it behind him and charged up the corridor. Three seconds later, a couple of shouted oaths that told Sebastian that Harry had not hit his head nearly hard enough.

There was a shout from an open doorway to his right and the dark shadow of a moving body, but Sebastian didn't stop to investigate. He hurled himself up two flights of stairs and into the bathroom, threw himself back at the door and turned the key.

Under the sash window was a short slope of higgledy tiles, but there was no time to worry about falling, not with heavy footsteps out in the corridor and a fierce rattling at the door. Sebastian heaved up the sash as far as it would go, swung one leg out and then ducked down and forced out the other.

There were a series of thumps behind him: someone was battering down the door. He let go of the window frame and slid, crouching precariously, down the tiles. But now his feet were slipping away from him–now he was out of control–and here under his nose was the precipitous emptiness at the bottom of the roof.

He overbalanced and fell head first into the void.

There was no time to think: he pushed with his feet as he left the roof and, just as instinctively, he grabbed at the first thing that came within reach.

There was a tremendous jolt as his weight nearly wrenched his arm off and he lost his grip. But he'd swerved in the air, somehow and now he was a split second away from something huge and appallingly solid. He crashed into it with an encircling *boing,* found himself sliding, got his jumper snagged on something, grabbed at a rusty edge, managed to swing a little and grabbed with his other hand, too. He took two huge gasping breaths, swallowed down his pneumatic-drilling heart and realized he was dangling under the boom of a crane.

Something heavy hit the metal beside him with a *tang* and a scrape of paint and Sebastian remembered the statue of Ora that had been on the bathroom windowsill. Sebastian suddenly realized how soft his flesh and bones were and that got him moving again. He squirmed swiftly round to the far side of the boom and let himself drop the last six feet. His legs were running before he'd hit the ground.

And that was what he had to do. Run and dodge down every turning that presented itself: lose the men behind him in the jumble of little turnings. But run. That was the main thing.

He mustn't stop thinking, though: he had to get away from the building site, or he might find himself trapped by a chasm in the earth or by a pile of crumbling spoil.

Dodge, twist. Keep moving, moving.

The hill was all Temple land, so why didn't he know it better? Where was he?

Just keep moving.

Or was this a dead end?

Can't take the risk. Run.

Noises ahead, now, but not mechanical noises. Not building work, another noise.

What?

Keep moving.

Daylight ahead–proper open daylight–a way out, it must be.

Run for it.

Yes – a main street. A main, broad street, with nowhere to hide: but there was nowhere else to go.

Sebastian ran out of the alley into the bright sunshine and straight into something soft.

He bounced and fell and found himself peering up past a bulging belly to a dazzling placard that said: FREEDOM FROM ANARCHY.

'Oof!' the man said; and then Sebastian muttered

'Sorry,' picked himself up and dived into the crowd.

There were thousands of people shuffling and jostling together as they walked uphill. Sebastian ducked and squeezed and elbowed his way through against the great current of people. He couldn't go fast, but at least there were perhaps twenty broad backs between him and the dangerous eyes of Mr Meeno's gang now. Sebastian desperately needed everything to stop for a couple of minutes, so he could get his breath back and work out where he was going: but he didn't dare stop. The men behind him would be fanning out and taking side-turnings, looking to head him off and –

'*Darling?*'

There was a lady in front of him bearing a placard which read 'DEMO FOR DEMOCRACY'.

'Excuse me,' muttered Sebastian, stooping down under her elbow.

'*Sebastian!*'

He recognized his mother at second glance. He paused for a second, blinking and confused, but then he went to plunge on.

'*You* can't march, you idiot!' said a glossy-haired girl at his elbow. It was Eunice, uplifted and fiercely joyful. Her placard read: 'BOOKS NOT COOKS'. 'You'd be protesting against yourself!'

Sebastian risked a swift backward glance. They were still following him, conspicuous in their dark suits amongst the sea of T-shirts and denim.

'Got to go,' he muttered, dodging round to put his family between him and the nearest suit, but someone caught hold of him. It was Robert, of course.

'But what are you doing here?' asked Mrs Blewitt.

The men hadn't spotted him yet. That was something. Sebastian might even have got clear away except that Robert was still clutching his arm. Sebastian squirmed, but Robert was much bigger than he was.

'Where do you think you're going?' asked Edward, peering round his 'MALLS NOT BALLS' placard, his glasses flashing in a way that would surely draw attention.

'There's some men trying to catch me,' said Sebastian, exasperated, but even then Robert didn't let go and the rest of them only looked puzzled. The crowd shuffled on and Sebastian had no choice but to go with them.

Harry was there, over there, standing up on an old mounting block where he got a perfect view of the whole crowd. He was scanning every person who went past. He had his hand held casually inside his jacket and Sebastian knew exactly why.

And there was Slats, up on the doorstep of a bookshop, squinting against the sun.

'You've got to let me go,' said Sebastian, urgently. 'There are some people over there and they're out to get me.'

'You haven't been singing during Offerings again, have you?' asked Robert, with a snigger and the only thing that stopped Sebastian braining him was the knowledge that it would make him horribly conspicuous.

'No,' he said. 'Look, I've discovered what Mr Meeno's gang's up to. That's why they want to get rid of me.'

'Who, darling?' asked Mrs Blewitt, but Mr Blewitt's glasses were suddenly sweeping the crowd and they were taking in Harry and Slats.

Mr Blewitt murmured a word that even Sebastian kept for special occasions.

'All right,' he said, quietly, but with a quite new decision, 'we'll go down Blessed Street and hope to lose them.' He took Mrs Blewitt's placard from her and presented it to a pink man in a lumberjack shirt.

'But whatever –' began Mrs Blewitt, but Mr Blewitt had already taken her firmly by the elbow and was steering her through the crowd.

It wasn't possible to hurry without disturbing the steady, relentless flow of the crowd. The most they could do was shuffle gradually sideways. Sebastian tried to keep his head down, but he could feel Harry and Slats perched above the people like deadly vultures.

'I think Eunice and Robert and Edward had better stay with the march,' said Mr Blewitt, suddenly. 'And you, too, dear. I'm rather afraid this may be dangerous.'

'Oh no, darling,' said Mrs Blewitt. 'Not if you might be dealing with those awful people. You aren't nearly assertive enough. I knew you should have done that Self-Empowerment course.'

But Mr Blewitt shook his head.

'I'm not sure they'd stop to listen to me, dear,' he said. 'Well, everyone who's coming had better come. Don't hurry. Robert, let Sebastian in front of you so you can shield him.'

'What?' said Robert, indignantly. 'So I'm between Sebastian and Mr Meeno's gang? Shield him from what?'

'Shield him from view,' said Mr Blewitt.

Blessed Street was half in grey shadow and half in glaring sunshine. The Blewitts eased their way out of the crowd and allowed themselves to melt into the shadows.

'Sebastian,' said Mr Blewitt, 'where's the best place to go? Should we go home?'

Sebastian thought about the Blewitts' large windows

and flimsy doors.

'We'd be safer in the Temple, I think.'

'They don't know your name? Who you are?'

Sebastian shook his head.

'Down here, then,' said Mr Blewitt. 'One at a time and quietly, please.'

Robert gave a mocking laugh.

'What is this? Peek-a-boo?'

But there was an uneasy note to his laughter.

They took a couple of turnings and then suddenly Sebastian knew where he was.

'We can cut down this way,' he said.

'But–'

'Side-entrance.'

Turville opened the door to them. In the shadow of the doorway his pale face looked even whiter than usual.

'Came back early,' explained Sebastian, gruffly. 'Something cropped up.'

But still Turville stood, white-faced, in the doorway: and Sebastian had to admit that the sight of the Blewitts *en masse* was enough to put the wind up anyone.

'This is my family,' he admitted, rather reluctantly. 'It's all right; they won't be staying long.'

But then a voice spoke from the darkness behind Turville.

'That's just where you're wrong,' it said.

Chapter 43

Sebastian recognized the voice even before Harry's face loomed out of the dimness.

'Everyone inside,' he snarled. 'Get moving!'

Mr Blewitt put a hand on Eunice's and Mrs Blewitt's shoulders and guided them in carefully. Jerome and Slats were waiting for them.

'Well, really!' said Mrs Blewitt. 'This is *quite* unacceptable.'

'Hush, now, dear,' murmured Mr Blewitt. 'Sebastian, I thought you said they didn't know you.'

Turville swept back his hair tragically.

'Mr Walty told them,' he wailed. 'Poor man, he didn't know what he was doing–but when he heard the description of who was impersonating him of course he knew who it was straight away. Oh, and whatever will become of you all!'

Harry's lips curled.

'I do not believe that is something you wish to know,' he said and smiled nastily. 'Slats!'

'I'm here, Harry.'

'I'm faced with somewhat of a dilemma,' said Harry. 'OK we put the bag on the kid. But what about these other citizens?'

Slats resettled his jacket on his shoulders and bounced his golf ball a bit.

'We got to keep them quiet, Harry.'

'That, Slats, is most certainly the case. We got to keep them as quiet as the grave. Jerome!'

Jerome didn't exactly perk up, but something stirred beneath the thick slab of his face, like the heavings of a sleepy hippo in a swamp.

'Shall I hit them, Harry?' he asked, hopefully. 'That'd keep them quiet.'

Robert flushed and bunched his fists.

'I'll jolly well hit you back!' he said indignantly and Sebastian could hardly believe that anyone, even Robert, could be so stupid.

Eunice flung back her hair and put her hands on her hips.

'Now look here,' she said. 'Just who do you think you are?'

Harry smiled again, a smile that had spread fear and doom throughout a considerable portion of the inhabited world.

'I'm the guy with the mob, sweetheart,' he explained. 'So if I were you I'd show a little respect.'

'Oh!' said Eunice, sharply, as if he'd slapped her. She didn't show any obvious signs of respect, but she shut up, which was as much as anyone could hope for.

Edward snorted pettishly.

'But I don't *understand*,' he said. 'It's bad enough being dragged away from the demonstration, but now we're being held up by these people and I have no idea what it's all about.'

'It's just one of those things, I'm afraid, Edward,' said Mr Blewitt, apologetically. 'Nobody's fault, I'm sure.'

Robert rounded on his father.

'Nobody's fault?' he echoed. '*Nobody's fault?* You don't suppose it has anything to do with that little pest Sebastian, then?'

'Now, dear,' said Mrs Blewitt, practically, 'I do understand your resentment, but we mustn't let the situation run away with us. I think we should all and I mean all, take some time out to reflect, because I think this situation shows signs of falling into animosity.'

'Shall I hit her, Harry?'

'It's *always* Sebastian!' said Eunice.

'Now now,' said Mrs Blewitt, with her hands raised up rather as if she were carrying a very large parcel, which was supposed to call down peace and bliss on them all, 'that's rather an exaggeration, isn't it, dear.'

'An exaggeration?' snapped Robert, hotly. 'Eunice isn't exaggerating! All the evidence clearly indicates that whenever there's trouble, Sebastian's at the bottom of it. I –'

Crunch – WHACK!

Everybody leapt several inches into the air and came down with mosquitoes buzzing in their earholes.

In the shocked silence that followed, shards of pottery skittered about on the table. Harry tapped his blackjack meaningfully on his palm.

'OK,' said Harry, into the appalled silence when the bits of the shattered teapot had trembled their way to a standstill. 'That was a whack on the table. Just as a demonstration. But don't think I wouldn't administer a little light hair-combing to the next person who annoys me.'

Everyone had stopped talking. It was incredible: Sebastian had never, ever, in his whole life, known all the members of his family to stop talking at the same time, but Harry had done it.

'Slats! Find some rope!' ordered Harry.

'There's a ball of string in the cupboard in the hallway,' said Turville, 'second drawer on the left.' Then, when Robert and Eunice turned to glare at him, he went on: 'I just really don't want anyone getting hurt, dears.'

'That is one sensible man,' said Harry, nodding. 'Cooperation. That's what makes the world go round smoothly for all parties. You heard him, Slats. String!'

It was the hairy, prickly sort.

'Make a good job of it, OK, Slats?'

'Never lost one yet.'

Slats swung a chair into the centre of the room, pointed at the seat and said to Eunice:

'Ladies first.'

And Eunice went and sat on it. Sebastian could hardly believe it: Eunice, gabby Eunice, the bossiest person ever to draw breath, was allowing Slats to tie her to the chair.

Sebastian enjoyed it thoroughly: and Eunice's being gagged with a tea towel was an unexpected bonus.

'Oh no, not that one, dear,' said Turville. 'That's the one I use for polishing the kettle. Take a clean one from that drawer over there. Yes, that's better. I never did like that one very much. It was a present from the seaside and I've been trying to wear it out for absolute centuries. Never mind, my love,' he went on, soothingly, to Eunice. 'All those bright patterns bring out your colour.'

'Him next,' growled Harry.

Turville stepped forward brightly.

'Ooh, how thrilling. You know, I've never been tied up before. How do you want me?'

Slats knelt down to secure Turville's ankles, first. Mr and Mrs Blewitt were as palely green as Robert and Edward, but Turville, bless him, seemed to be quite enjoying it all.

Slats must have had wide experience at tying people up. He wound a loop twice round Turville's throat and tied the ends somewhere behind him.

'Now I would advise you not to struggle,' he said. 'Because struggling would be inclined to make the string round your neck tighter and that would not be compatible with breathing.'

'Oh, don't you worry,' said Turville, brightly. 'I'll be as good as gold. I promise.'

Slats paused in the act of walking away and then stretched out a spindly finger to touch the heavy gold chain that Turville was wearing round his neck.

'Nice,' he commented.

Turville smiled.

'Isn't it,' he agreed. 'It's one of my favourites. Hand-forged, you know, by a friend of mine ... what are you doing?'

Slats was pulling the chain through his fingers, searching for the catch.

'Oh dear,' said Turville, regretfully, 'you aren't thinking of taking it, are you? Because really I would advise against it. Really I would. I would be awfully upset.'

'Aw,' said Slats. 'Diddums.'

'And I,' said Turville, suddenly looking up into his face, 'would also be terribly cross. Really I would, Slats.'

Slats flinched as if someone had hit him, dropped the chain and went back to tightening the string round Turville's wrists.

'OK,' said Harry, a little later. 'All fixed up?'

'Yeah, Harry. That's the whole lot of them nice and snug, except for the Walty guy.'

'That's OK.' Harry jerked his head at Sebastian. 'He's coming with us.'

Sebastian took one last blissful look at his family, all in a row with tea towels tied round their mouths. It was marvellous–it was brilliant–and he couldn't think why he hadn't thought of wanting something like that before, perhaps as a birthday treat. Then Jerome enfolded his arm in a massive paw and led him away.

Chapter 44

They travelled in a long black limo with tinted windows. It swayed and rocked round the tight corners of the City, rumbling on the cobbles. They had to go the long way round, because of the demonstration, but there was hardly any traffic. The golden streets of the City slid past them, quite deserted and suddenly Sebastian found himself with an empty, cold feeling under his breastbone.

They got out outside the main entrance to Mr Meeno's offices.

'How long now?' asked Harry.

Slats consulted his watch.

'Twenty minutes.'

'OK. You two check out the trucks and I'll go report to the boss.'

Honey was still hitched up on the window sill of what had been Mr Meeno's office, but she had advanced to filing the nails on her right hand.

'Where's Meeno?' demanded Harry.

Honey shrugged pettishly.

'Where do you think? Down the hole. Say, what is it with you guys? I mean, I wouldn't say that this here city is the place where I'd want to spend my whole life – there ain't enough places of sophisticated entertainment for a girl like me – but it sure beats spending all my time down a nasty black hole.'

Harry snorted.

'Yeah,' he said. 'Well, you wouldn't understand.'

'Though,' she went on, 'at least the rats have gone. You did a good job, there, Mr Walty. Wonderful, it was, Harry. He just sort of whistled to them, only so high up you couldn't hear it.'

Harry gave Sebastian a shove that nearly sent him head-first into the tunnel.

It was a really good tunnel. Sebastian was extremely impressed. It had steps down and a knotted rope handrail and the electric lights were in cage-things to stop you burning yourself. Even Jerome could make his way down it if he adopted a low-armed gait that seemed quite natural to him and Sebastian only had to bend his knees a bit and watch out for his head.

'Cor,' he said. 'This is brilliant. It must have taken years to dig out all this.'

'Six weeks,' said Harry, gruff, but grudgingly pleased. 'And that's with all the heavy explosives being done just on Fridays.'

'Oh. Oh, yeah. Really clever, that is. How far does it go?'

'Shut your mouth. You'll soon find out.'

It seemed quite a long way, but it might only have

been fifty yards. It ended in an igloo-shaped room, hollowed out of the stony earth. Mr Meeno was there.

'You got him, Harry?'

'We got him.'

A head poked out of a jagged hole in the far wall.

'We're all set to go, boss,' it said, grinning like a gargoyle. 'We've fitted twenty seconds of spaghetti, just like you said.'

'That's good,' said Mr Meeno. 'Are you certain it's going to do the job?'

'Sure, boss,' said the head. 'We've got it all tucked up real snug and artistic.'

'Yeah,' said Mr Meeno. 'Well, go back and sing lullabies to it, OK? I'm busy.'

'OK, boss.'

Mr Meeno turned to view Sebastian. His eyes had glints in them like dirty ice.

'This Walty guy,' he said. 'He is a problem to me, Harry. The obvious thing is to put the sluggola on him and then dump him someplace where no one ain't going to find him until we're far away.'

Harry brightened a little.

'I know a good place, boss,' he offered.

'Sure you do, Harry. But that is not the problem. The problem is that he is only a small and junior member of society. And hitting a kid is a very immoral and wicked deed with which my organization has nothing to do. Why, I have even given my nephew Horace a home and victuals, even though he is the unluckiest, most ham-fisted kid I've ever come across, with a kisser that gave even his own mother nightmares.'

'But no one would know,' said Harry, reasonably. 'I've got all his family and his servant guy tied up in the back of the Temple. Turns out he's not called Walty after all: that was just a cover. He's the Blewitt beezer that hangs out in the Temple.'

Mr Meeno gave Sebastian a sharp glance and then he let out a long low whistle.

'The apprentice,' he murmured. 'Well, well, well. Well, well, well. And I didn't recognize him without his dress. Harry!'

'Yes, boss?'

'Harry, you are a great guy at the executive end of things, but you ain't subtle. You won't never be a prominent citizen unless you get subtle. Hit a guy, put a guy on ice – that is a very old-fashioned way of conducting business, Harry.'

'Guess so, boss.'

'You need to look at the big picture. All those councillors, priests, whatever: they never got to the top without standing back and looking at the big picture, hey, Harry?'

'Guess not, boss.'

'Now take the case in point. We are going to have plenty of heat on us after this job. There are going to be whole posses of gendarmes just twitching to discuss the enterprise, for we have shook up this place quite some and the citizens are naturally fond of peace and quiet.

'Now, if they're after us for re-distributing a few sacks of hot potatoes – stuff that no one's ever set eyes on, that's just been mouldering away down here for centuries doing no good – well, that's just a business transaction, ain't it? Anyone'd do it if they had the nerve and the organizational genius. Do you follow me?'

'Sure, boss.'

'But if we hit the kid – this kid, the Blewitt kid, who's in the papers every day of the week and who's been putting on entertainments for all the people–why then folk would regard us with horror and loathing and they wouldn't rest until they'd scoured the globe for our cosy retirement home, Harry, and made us a gift of a whole bunch of pineapples and caused an outbreak of fresh air through our bodies that'd make us dead more than somewhat.'

All through that speech something was happening. Sebastian wasn't exactly sure what it was, but it was sending cold bolts through his insides and shivering the hair on his arms and legs. And, although Sebastian didn't know what it was that was happening, he knew it was something terribly terribly important.

'Mr Meeno!' he said, suddenly almost unable to bear it.

It was something to do with the hoard. Sebastian didn't know how he knew, but he did.

'Kid?'

'Are you really going to steal the gold in Ora's vaults?' he said. 'Because I wouldn't.' He gulped as an extra strong bolt of danger shot shudderingly through him. 'Really and truly, I wouldn't.'

'Oh yeah?'

'Yeah,' said Sebastian and the overpowering sense of catastrophe was beating on him from all sides. 'Because ... because –'

But he didn't know why. He just knew, absolutely knew that something terrible and all-engulfing would happen if Mr Meeno did.

Mr Meeno laid a fatherly hand on his shoulder.

'Hey, it's no big deal,' he said. 'It's just a whole heap of gold that's been lying around for thousands of years doing no good to nobody. Why, no one's even *set eyes on* the gold in there for more years than anyone can remember. It's not even as if there's going to be anyone to miss it. All I'm going to do is take the gold somewhere where the sun can shine on it and make people very happy. Don't you think that's a fine thing to do?'

It was a fine thing to do: Sebastian would have been quite ready to hail it as a stroke of genius and then start haggling for a share of the loot, if only it weren't for the terrible feeling inside him that was chilling his bones and his blood and all of the rest of him right to the tips of his ears.

'It's the nest of Ora,' he blurted out, but without knowing where the words had come from. 'You mustn't disturb the nest of Ora.'

Mr Meeno smiled indulgently.

'Sure, sure, you're professionally involved with the Temple,' he said. 'I can see where you're coming from, kid. But, hey, look at it from my point of view. This Ora – I can see that He's a popular guy round these parts, but I can't say I've ever met Him personally. And, I'll tell you something else: I've done business with the High Priest and with all sorts of the guys who work round this metropolis, but I guess I've never met anyone who *has* met Him. Now, I'm a peaceful sort of guy and I wouldn't want to cause despondency or cynicism in anyone, but, I've kind of got the idea that this Ora is a quiet, retiring sort of guy who isn't going to be too fussed what happens. I mean, what does an immortal god want with a heap of gold?'

Sebastian took a deep wavering breath. He knew the answer to that, but the terror that was filling that domed space as surely as a rising flood left him with no attention spare to work it out.

'Hey! You in there!'

'Boss?' said the head, making a sudden reappearance.

'Light the fuse.'

'OK, boss. Here goes. Put your fingers in your ears.'

'Oh, help,' gulped Sebastian. He didn't know how it had happened, but something had clenched his stomach into a cold hard knot and something else had taken all the muscles out of his arms and legs and replaced them with iced spaghetti. Just a little bit of him was full of glorious excitement at the thought of the biggest firework ever, but the rest of him was breathless with a conviction of absolute disaster.

The head reappeared in the hole and this time its body scrambled after it.

'Heads down!' it shouted and threw itself on its face by the far wall. Sebastian crouched down and put up his arms to cover his head and his stomach did a clumsy back-flop that almost heaved up his breakfast.

The floor pushed sharply against his feet. Sebastian found himself toppling forwards over a wave of sulphurous air and he landed on his hands, did a forward roll and landed somewhere where the lights had gone out. Things were falling on him – bits of earth, probably – and then something heavier, sharper, like a stone.

He cried out, but the blare of the explosion was storming through the chamber, swiping aside everything it met and any noise he made was obliterated, utterly. The noise came in a solid wave that punched at Sebastian's eardrums. He lay with his arms over his head and waited and waited for the tons of earth that made up the roof to fall and crush him into the ground. And then the wave was somehow more of a noise than a pain and he realized that it was very gradually fading, like a receding tide.

Soon there was only a fierce buzzing in his ear and then finally silence. Sebastian waited until things had stopped falling on his head and then he ventured to push himself up.

The chamber was quite a lot bigger than before. The floor was ankle-deep in chunks of rock and lumps of earth and the cage that had held the light bulb was dangling in tangled ruin. But through the billowing clouds of dust there was a light. Not a flickering light, like a fire, or a cold steady light, like a light bulb, but something warm, glowing, soft.

The dust was beginning to settle, now. Sebastian could see, black against the glow, twisted iron bars as thick as his arm that poked out their sharp broken ends into the chamber.

And past the bars, gleaming through the dust-swirling air, there was gold. Acres of it. A great cavern filled to the roof with gold that stretched further than could be seen. Warm, enticing, opulent; stacked in deep-stamped ingots or wrinkled pebbles or shining statuettes. No jewels: nothing but soft, pure gold stretching into dimness.

'The biggest heist in the world,' said a ragged figure beside him, reverently, in the voice of Mr Meeno.

And then from behind them another voice said:

'*Now* you've done it.'

Chapter 45

There was a figure in the chamber that had not been there before. It was more than man-size, although its head fitted comfortably below what remained of the roof. Its body was slender and delicately muscled and it was naked except for a golden cloth around its loins and a fall of chains that shone against the softer gold of its chest.

Sebastian's heart lurched so massively he only just managed to gulp it down. 'Ora,' he said, in wonder.

Ora smiled down at him. His tiger eyes disappearing for a moment in a slow blink.

'Of course, sweetheart,' He said, gently. 'How nice to see you. You're not hurt, are you?'

Dumbly, Sebastian shook his head.

'That's very good. Now, my love, creep behind a pile of rock or something, there's a good boy, while I blast the perpetrators of this awful sacrilege.'

Mr Meeno was heaving himself to his feet and brushing the dust off the sleeves of his suit.

'Now hold on a gold-digging minute,' he said. 'Let's get a few things straight round here.'

'Yes,' said Ora, with a certain feline mildness, turning the light of His tawny eyes upon him. 'Let's.'

Mr Meeno shot his cuffs and went on, a little

aggressively, almost as if he wasn't terrified out of his wits. Which was completely crazy.

'I don't know how you got in here,' he said, scowling, 'but this is by way of being a private enterprise and visitors are not welcome. Got me?'

Ora blinked, again and something warm went out of the place. Sebastian, on the ground, found himself shivering.

'Ah yes,' said Ora, thoughtfully. 'You are Meeno. The boss. You came to the Temple, didn't you? You even brought me an Offering, once.'

'Yeah, that's right,' said Mr Meeno. 'You were welcome. But now I'm on private business and–'

'– and this is a private hoard,' said Ora, steadily, almost gently: almost, but not quite, kindly. 'And I'm afraid I'm not sharing.'

A heap of rubble stirred, groaned, shook itself and turned into Harry.

'Neither are we,' he snarled. And in his hands were two wires, glinting coldly through the golden dust.

'Look out!' Sebastian yelled and threw himself back down on his face. There was a huge, ear-battering explosion and more stones came down on Sebastian's head, but Sebastian hardly noticed. All he was thinking about was that Ora hadn't thrown Himself down onto the floor with the others: and that meant the golden figure would have caught the full force of the blast.

His heart hurt, suddenly, as if he'd been injured himself: and he decided that he was going to kill them all.

He raised his head – and then Sebastian felt all the breath go out of him. Ora was still standing, but the gleaming smoothness of His golden skin was wounded, punctured. He'd been blown backwards by the blast and one of the broken bars had driven itself deep through Ora's chest. Sebastian scrambled to his feet.

'I'll get an ambulance,' he said. 'I'll run all the way, don't you worry. I'll find a phone. Just hold on, all right?'

But Ora smiled a golden smile and Sebastian felt a sudden warmth, an instant glow of certainty and he felt no need to move.

'It's all right, sweetheart,' said Ora, gently. 'It's just a wound. Soon mended.'

And before their eyes the ugly flaps of skin closed like flowers in the summer dusk and the god of the City was whole again.

'Cor,' said everybody, softly and in awe.

Mr Meeno was the first to recover himself. He smoothed back his hair.

'But on the other hand,' he said, 'seeing as the circumstances are somewhat unusual, I may see my way to making a deal.'

Ora flicked him a tiger glance; warm, but full of more power than existed in the world.

'All right,' He said, calmly. 'I'll make you an offer. You put the wall of my nest back and I'll let you out of here alive. How about that?'

Sebastian reckoned that was the best offer Mr Meeno had had in a very long time. But Mr Meeno showed no signs of falling on his knees and giving thanks. Instead he took his cigar from behind his ear, blew off the dust and put it in his mouth.

'Fifty-fifty,' he said. But Ora only smiled, slightly, but very beautifully and shook His head.

And in that moment Sebastian was overtaken by a feeling of intense familiarity. It was Ora, of course, and he'd seen pictures of Him since he was a baby. He was just like the statue in the Temple that Sebastian saw every day.

The statue was a really good likeness, Sebastian decided. It caught the curve of the trunk and the tilt of the head.

But there was something else about Ora, this Ora before him, that was even more familiar than that. There was something about His voice, the way He moved, that was somehow as familiar as toast.

'No,' said Ora, in His never-before-heard but utterly familiar golden voice. 'It's all mine. It's what is left of the love of all the people and it has been here for many many years. Even when someone fails and leaves the world and returns to be part of me, then their gifts stay with me and I stay with them. My hoard is the most precious thing in the whole universe. And the universe, Mr Meeno, is a large and precious place.'

And still Mr Meeno did not go down on his knees and worship Ora. Instead he spread out his hands.

'Look,' he said, somehow managing to seem quite reasonable. 'I can see your point of view. But I've made a large investment over this gold. Loads of guys, they told me it was a fairy tale, that I was on a wild-goose chase, but I always believed in it, right from when I was a kid like my nephew Horace, only a lot smarter and not so ugly. Now, you wouldn't want to rob me and my associates of the fruits of our labours, would you?'

But the god of the universe only laughed.

'You people,' He said. 'You are so entertaining, all of you. I could never ever leave you, or make you perfect.'

'Entertaining?' echoed Mr Meeno and now there was a dangerous glint in his eye. 'That was not entertainment, that was a serious proposition.'

'Oh, I know,' said Ora. 'I could tell. I can do this mind-reading thing, you see. Yes, I know all your secrets, Mr Meeno. Yes, even that one. And that one and well may you look ashamed of yourself. But I'll tell you what

I'll do. Because you haven't hurt my small friend here (whom I have loved very much for some time, now), I'm going to let you out of here with whole skins. Yes, even you, Harry, and I hope you realize that it's far more than you deserve. In fact, my original impulse was to throw you into the gold-refining crucibles – but there! To be quite honest I'm not really in a hurry to have even the perfect part of you – small and very nearly insignificant as it is – in my heart.'

'Now look here –' began Mr Meeno, scowling; but Ora swept on magnificently.

'I'll even let you keep the ill-gotten gains that are packed in the lorries – even Honey, I think; she is far too good for you, but she would be unhappy if you were parted. But not Horace. No, not Horace. It's true that he's very nearly the least attractive person in the City and that he's spent nearly all his time just lately trying to murder my apprentice here, but I do feel he deserves the chance to grow up with someone who will provide a better example.'

'Now just you wait a minute –'

'So,' said Ora, unperturbably, 'the only thing to decide is just what to do with you. The tidiest solution would be to put you in the river with your business acquaintances, but I don't think I want your bones in my City, Mr Meeno.'

'Now you look here –'

'So I think I'll send you somewhere that's really quite a long way away, in planetary terms, where you can't do any more harm. Ah! Ah, yes. Now I come to think about it, I know just the place. Goodbye, Mr Meeno.'

Mr Meeno put his hands on his hips: squat, square and scowling.

'Hey,' he said. 'Now just you wait a –'

But Ora raised an elegant wrist and flicked his fingers and Mr Meeno wasn't there any more.

Sebastian blinked several times, but Mr Meeno was definitely not there and Harry was gone too and so was the head. The only people left among the softly gold-hued rubble were Sebastian and the great golden figure of Ora Himself.

'Cor,' said Sebastian, hoarsely and Ora smiled again.

'And now, sweetheart,' he said. 'For my beautiful nest.'

He raised a hand gracefully, languidly, as if pointing to a view; but the muscles beneath his golden skin slid and swelled with power.

And the iron bars began to writhe. They twisted and turned like snakes, seeking out their partners, joining mouths and pushing each other away into perfect rigidity and straightness. And then Sebastian was putting up his arms to shield his head again because the air was full of bits of rubble that were leaping up off the floor all around him. None of them touched him, but as Sebastian jumped out of the way of one bit he landed on a stone and found himself whizzing up towards the roof with the force of its rising.

Ora clicked his fingers and every clod of earth and mote of dust was instantly arrested in the air. Sebastian let out the lungful of air he'd taken in to yell and jumped down off the stone that'd zoomed his head nearly up to the roof. He looked around carefully for two empty bits of floor for his feet.

'Keep still, my love,' said Ora's golden voice. 'It won't hurt you. I promise.'

And with the tiniest twitch of his finger the earth continued fitting itself impossibly together into a tightly-packed jigsaw that turned into a solid wall. Even the whitewash from the wall re-assembled itself so that not a crack showed.

'Cor,' said Sebastian, again and this time Ora smiled a full shining smile that cast a light all round the room, so that Sebastian even felt it deep inside himself, comforting and satisfying, like treacle pudding on a frosty day.

'We'd better get out of here, now,' said Ora, kindly. 'I'm going to fill in the tunnel and block off the bookcase again. There's no point in putting temptation within people's reach, particularly if it involves my hoard.'

And again Sebastian was teased by that feeling of

almost recognition. It was Ora, just like the statue in the Temple, but as well it was – He shook his head and followed Ora along the tunnel and up to what had once been Mr Meeno's study. And although Sebastian still had to stoop a little, Ora walked through upright, even though he was at least seven or eight feet tall.

It was very confusing.

Honey was gone. Sebastian felt a bit regretful about that, because there'd been nothing wrong with Honey that a few brains wouldn't have put right.

But Ora shook His head and smiled His warm smile again.

'It's all right, my love, she's quite happy,' he said. 'I've sent her and Mr Meeno to a rather nice oasis in the middle of a beautiful big desert: lots of bananas and everything. Honey will like it there: she'll have lots of children who will love her very much and Mr Meeno will be kept very busy growing food for them all.'

Sebastian wondered what had happened to the others.

'Oh, I've split them up. They're all rather weak-spirited creatures, really and I doubt they'll have the gumption to make much trouble by themselves. Not since they've had the honour of seeing me in all my glory, at any rate.'

And if it hadn't been Ora, you might have thought there was a trace of a smugness about His face as He said that.

'You know, my love,' he continued, 'I don't really have much of a taste for being god-like – ironic, isn't it, given the circumstances – but the world feels better already for their being broken up, doesn't it.'

Sebastian couldn't feel anything different at all, but there was something about being alone with an impossibly golden god that inclined him to keep his mouth shut.

Ora fixed His beautiful tiger eyes on the space behind the bookcase.

'You'd better put your fingers in your ears, dear,' he advised. 'Because I'm going to be god-like again. Rather vulgar, but there it is. Ready? Then: *abracadabra hey presto kazoom*!'

Solid rock. That was what it was. One moment, space containing safe and tunnel and the next, rough, natural, untouched-by-human-hand rock. You could even see the stripes where it'd been laid down over thousands and millions of years.

'Cor!' said Sebastian, again, fervently and Ora licked a finger with a glistening tawny tongue and smoothed an already perfect eyebrow.

'Actually, it's rather nice to stretch my powers,' He admitted. 'I mean, it is *vulgar*, but sometimes I wonder whether I might have an obligation to punish malefactors. I have done it, from time to time; but then,

I expect you've learned all about that from Mr Walty, haven't you?'

Sebastian found himself struggling to swallow a brick that had suddenly got caught in his throat. If the Sacred Texts were to be believed (and this was not the moment for doubting them) then this was the being who'd once turned a High Priest into a turkey for getting above himself in the matter of hats.

What would Ora do to an apprentice who'd been making up his own laws?

'Ah, yes,' said Ora, reflectively, 'but then Gurdlepod was ever such a long time ago and the hat business was the final straw. He really was ever such an unpleasant, nasty, selfish old man: everyone was ever so pleased when I did it and he did make ever so much better a turkey than he ever did a High Priest.'

Sebastian just found himself kind of wondering what sort of animal the current High Priest might be good at being, but then he stopped thinking about it quickly, in case he should be giving Ora ideas.

He was too late. Ora frowned a little.

'Yes,' he said, thoughtfully. 'A whale, probably: he could sing all day and never be afraid of anyone. But the thing is that you're all so lovely as you are, you see, you little humans. You're such fun and so interesting, even if you're not anywhere near perfect, even on a good day with the light behind you. That's really why I decided on a policy of non-interference. So I'm not sure I should do anything with him. What do you think?'

Several amusing ideas sprang to Sebastian's mind, the best of which was turning every drink that touched the High Priest's lips to barley-water. But then he thought again, more seriously.

'He's only really got into all this trouble because he's had Mr Meeno frightening him,' he said. 'You can't blame him for going to pieces, really. The thing is,' he went on, scowling ferociously with the effort of thinking, 'he's not really the right type to be High Priest. He's too wishy-washy. He gets bored and lonely and then all he can think of to do is eat and drink.'

And at that Ora's whole magnificent body glowed in a burst of joy.

'I'll appoint him a personal trainer,' he said. 'That's what he needs. And someone watching his diet.'

'Turville would do that,' said Sebastian, helpfully, in awe at the thought of the High Priest on early morning jogs. 'He's brilliant, Turville is.'

Ora smiled a wide and splendid smile and stretched up His arms lazily through the ceiling, but without causing any damage at all to the plaster. Ora's teeth were golden, but somehow milky white at the same time.

'I must say it does have its satisfactions, punishing people,' He observed. 'It's been such centuries that it'd rather gone out of my mind. I'd quite convinced myself that it was best to let all you humans muddle your way through, but, you know, I think that in this case I should perhaps have stepped in earlier. People have been bringing my name into disrepute.' He flicked a sideways, tiger-stone glance at Sebastian and then He went on: 'Haven't they, Sebastian, my love?'

Sebastian felt himself flush a fiery and uncomfortable red.

'I mean, those laws you were making up, dear. *Not* very sensible, really, were they?'

Sebastian gulped and thought again about turkeys.

'I'm really really sorry,' he said.

'So I see. Oh, my love, don't worry. I mean, what would I do without you? I do like to see a bit of life and happiness and my hoard has grown like anything since you introduced the singing ladies. Oh, and I do like to see the children watching the puppet show. Their little faces! And, anyway,' Ora went on, 'if I got rid of *you*, I'd have to choose another apprentice, wouldn't I? And who would I end up getting breakfast for every day then?'

Sebastian, startled, looked up at Ora and suddenly the teasing sense of recognition inside himself crystallized, and Sebastian recognized Him beyond any shadow of a doubt. Sebastian hadn't been used to seeing him eight feet tall and golden, but it was Him, all the same.

'Turville,' he said, in wonder.

Chapter 46

The god of the universe lowered His beautiful eyelashes in a slow, tiger-like blink.

'But of course,' He said.

'But –'

'Why not? After all, it's no good having pets if you don't look after them, is it? You should know that. Think of Gerald.'

Sebastian kept opening his mouth, but each time he did, his voice shrivelled in his throat.

Ora passed a golden finger under Sebastian's chin and Sebastian smelt the sweet scent of warm honey. And he was filled both with fear and with a fleeting feeling as if he was growing, sprouting shoots of life that combined him with everything that was beautiful in the whole of everything.

'I might not have stepped in at all if it hadn't been for Gerald,' said the golden voice, musingly. 'You showed me the way, really, my love. When Gerald started suffering, you stepped in, didn't you, to help him … It's tricky, though, especially when you can see everything that might happen. Still, I never thought it was going to be simple. It isn't what I want, anyway, for things to be simple.'

Sebastian was still so utterly amazed he could hardly breathe. Turville. Ora. Turville. *Turville*?

'Actually, I think it's all worked out very well,' said Ora, with a certain complacency. 'We'll be able to have your father's new shopping centre, now, nicely within walking distance of the Temple. Ooh, I will enjoy that. And poor Horace and dear Mrs Poash will find one another, I'm quite certain: and what fun *they'll* have, squabbling. And your father will get his job back, of course.'

'But –' began Sebastian. 'But ... but ... but why are you Turville?'

Ora raised a perfectly beautiful eyebrow.

'Well, why not?' he said. 'If I'm to be here and be with you all, then I've got to be someone, after all. It's ever so hard to get to know people properly if you're many feet tall and really ever so obviously God. And being a large golden waterfall is even worse. It draws crowds, for one thing and that's the last thing you want if you've just popped down the road for a packet of digestives. Anyway, I like being Turville: I get to spend lots of time in the Temple and I think that when people come to talk to me it's only polite to be there in person, isn't it. I never did like answer-phones. And being Turville means I'm close to my nest and I get to watch everything that's going on in a really human way. And I know everybody, but at the same time I'm just Turville, you understand; I mean, nobody has ever noticed that I've been opening doors to people for hundreds and hundreds of years. Which reminds me: I've left all your family tied up in the kitchen. We'd better be going home, Your Knowingness.'

It took no time at all. Sebastian blinked and worked out where he was and then he looked at the person standing next to him and it was Turville.

Sebastian looked at him really properly for the first time ever.

'I should have guessed,' he said. 'All those gold bracelets. And being able to arrange anything in the whole world.'

Sebastian took a long deep breath and realized that things were never going to be the same again. It was never going to be comfortable to receive his morning toast from an immortal god who could zap the life out of the universe in the blink of one perfect eye.

But Turville smiled and shook his head.

'Don't worry, sweetheart,' he said. 'You'll soon stop bothering about it.'

Sebastian opened his mouth and then he closed it again.

'I'm just going to disappear, my love,' said Turville.

'I've left a sort of shadow-thing asleep in the kitchen in my place. I'll just go and slip into it and then you can come in and set us all free.'

'But, Turville!' blurted Sebastian. 'I mean ... I mean, Ora ... your Godness ... I mean –'

'It's all right, sweetheart,' said Turville, gently and he vanished, leaving behind him nothing but a waft of honey-scented air.

Sebastian took another deep breath and turned to push open the door.

And there were all his family, seated in a line, tied up and gagged and all trying to gabble out instructions at once.

And all they could say was *mmmmmm*.

Sebastian stood and surveyed them with extreme pleasure and if it hadn't been the express order of the almighty god of the temple he really didn't think he could have brought himself to untie them.

It was just as he'd known it would be: as soon as each mouth was free it started jabbering. Luckily by the time all the Blewitts had the use of their mouths there were too many people talking at once to have a clue what any of them were saying. The worst one was Mrs Blewitt. Not only did she jabber and jabber and jabber, but she kept trying to hug Sebastian and with the room so crowded it was quite difficult to dodge.

The noise was so incredible that he ducked down under the table, in the end, to get away from the lot of them. He squatted gloomily under the fluffy tablecloth – and it was only then that he realized that the noise really was *incredible*. As well as the shrill yapping of his family there was a deeper, roaring sort of a noise and a dull thumping. And it was coming from somewhere outside.

Sebastian crawled out and made for the door to the corridor via the back of the saucepan cupboard. The rest of the family were having a five-way hug, so he got away unnoticed.

The roaring and thumping got louder as he went along the corridor. When he pushed open the door to the Temple itself he found that every golden lamp was ringing wincingly and that a sort of shadow of the great noise was being batted from one wall of the Temple to another, like a ceaseless and escalating game of catch.

Sebastian walked down between the golden chairs. He could feel his insides quivering and his teeth were fizzing in sympathy with the trembling lamps. He reached the main door, heaved at the golden barley-sugar handle and looked out.

The whole world was full of faces.

They were gazing up at the Temple, a milling mass of them. The whole square was filled with multi-coloured figures, so many of them that even the side streets were bright with the overspill, like a rag-rug octopus that was squeezing itself oozingly nearer to the Temple.

And suddenly, for the first time ever, the Temple felt to Sebastian like a fragile thing, like a bubble of filigree over an expanse of nothing.

Sebastian stepped back hastily and let the door sigh shut again. He was filled with the deepest dismay. Those faces: they were all wrong. They hadn't been filled with excitement or purpose, reverence or curiosity, like the faces that usually came up the steps to the Temple. They hadn't been filled –

Yes. That was the really important thing: they hadn't been filled with hope.

The crowd outside – the people – were chanting 'Down with the Temple' as they stamped on the golden flagstones of the square.

Sebastian slipped backwards into the main body of the Temple. He thought fleetingly about going to find the High Priest, but that was never going to be much use, so instead he ran back through the trembling Temple, through fantastically beautiful blizzards of somersaulting gold dust, to his quarters.

His family were still being shrill, but Turville was pouring out nice cups of soothing tea for everyone.

'There's a huge crowd of people outside,' Sebastian told him, rather breathlessly. 'They're shouting "Down with the Temple!"'

'Oh dear,' said Turville, tranquilly. 'People, nowadays.'

Mrs Blewitt blinked at him through the steam from her teacup.

'Thank heavens there's a back door,' she said. 'It's all right, everyone: don't worry. We can slip down past the market and get safely out of the way.'

Sebastian stared at her in amazement.

'*Safely out of the way*?' he echoed. 'We can't leave the Temple!'

Mrs Blewitt patted his arm.

'I know it's all been terribly traumatic, darling,' she said, 'and I'll book us all in for counselling first thing tomorrow, but I'm quite sure we'll be all right. The crowd will be too busy in the Temple to bother about us.'

Sebastian was more shocked still.

'I know,' he said. 'But we can't just go off and leave the Temple, can we?'

Mr Blewitt gave a rather grim smile, but Mrs Blewitt only stroked Sebastian's arm and gazed tragically into his eyes.

'I'm afraid that crowds can be very nasty things, darling. They might start throwing things about. Vandalizing things.'

'I know,' said Sebastian. 'Of course they will. So we can't go off and leave it, can we?'

'But, darling –'

'Can we, huh? I mean, it's the Temple of Ora, isn't it? Just about the most famous building in the whole world, isn't it? Just about the most *important* building in the whole world, too. Isn't it, huh? Isn't it?'

'Yes, of course,' said Mrs Blewitt. 'But –'

'So we can't just leave it to be smashed up, can we? Can we? Can we?'

Robert snorted.

'So just what do you propose to do about it?' he demanded. 'Fight them all back with your bare hands?'

'Robert!' said Mrs Blewitt, quickly. 'Don't put ideas into Sebastian's head!'

The noise of the crowd swayed louder and then, instead of receding, swayed louder again.

'They've reached the steps,' said Edward, tightly. 'If we don't go now –'

'You take the children, dear,' said Mr Blewitt, suddenly. 'I'll stay with Sebastian.'

Mrs Blewitt swung round on him, opened her mouth and then for the first time ever she didn't know what to say.

'Thanks,' said Sebastian, doughtily. 'But I need you all here. All of you.'

They all looked at each other and then at Sebastian.

'Need us?' asked Eunice. 'But what for?'

'To save the Temple,' said Sebastian, simply. 'Robert!'

Robert raised his haughtiest eyebrow.

'What?'

'You and Edward grab a couple of those grapefruit each and come with me.'

Eunice and Mrs Blewitt squeaked and rolled their eyes, but they loved it, really. It was the sequins: all girls loved sequins, especially when they were sewn onto shiny little vests. Edward and Robert weren't quite so keen, but it didn't matter: with the grapefruit, a few slashes of slimy lipstick and a couple of feathery turbans, from a distance you could quite easily take them for girls, as long as there was low lighting and lots of dry ice.

'There,' said Turville, busily patting blusher on Edward. 'Almost perfect, dear.'

'But I still don't see what good this is going to do,' said Robert, flushed and irritable under his false eyelashes.

'There have to be four dancers,' said Sebastian, sturdily. 'Two's not enough: it looks mingy and we can't have that if all that lot are going to take any notice of us. Dad!'

'I don't think I'd fit into the costume,' said Mr Blewitt, hastily. 'Anyway, I don't think I'd be very convincing with my beard, do you?'

'No,' said Sebastian, 'but I need you for technical support. I need dry ice – lots of it, to hide Robert– and gongs. All the big gongs. Start us off with tape 36 on full volume and then you four dance, sort of swaying, with your arms held up to the statue of Ora, bless His holy name and then Eunice starts singing.'

'Singing what?' asked Eunice, buckling golden bells to her ankles while she waited for Edward to finish painting his toenails.

'Anything, as long as it's loud,' said Sebastian. 'Just "Ora Ora Ora" will do. Just make it sound spooky and wave your arms about. With any luck we'll have deafened them with the music and the gongs and so they won't hear it anyway.'

'Thank you,' said Eunice, stiffly.

'I'm sure it'll be lovely, darling,' said Mrs Blewitt.

'And then,' said Sebastian, 'I'll pop up out of the dry ice and talk to them.'

'Great. And *then* they'll tear the place apart,' said Robert, cuttingly.

Sebastian shook his head.

'Not once I've explained,' he said. 'Not once I've shown them.'

'Shown them what, darling?' asked Mrs Blewitt.

Sebastian grinned.

'Gerald,' he said. 'I'm going to show them Gerald.'

Chapter 47

The ragged surge of the crowd pushed its way through the doors of the Temple and paused. Sebastian had switched out all the lights except for one spotlight focused on the statue. It took quite a while for the crowd's eyes to adjust and that slowed them down, just as Sebastian had intended. The golden dust shimmered before them, twirling and falling and on the pillars the golden bees were frozen in their perpetual quest for treasure.

And in the middle of the great space, the eyes of the great statue saw everything. It saw Finley, cap firmly on his head. It saw the whole of Mr Walty's class, released from school and full of delirious daring at being on a protest march; it saw Councillor Kimber and the rest of the Council; it saw Mrs Poash and all the vergers forming a brave thin line at its feet. It even saw, though this was behind it, the moist, anxious face of the High Priest peering out from the door to his private apartments.

The pressure from behind pushed at them all and they spilled forward. But they trod softly and none of them stamped on the gold-swirled tiles that cooled their tired feet.

Sebastian waited until the first of them were nearly

at the offering steps and then he signed to Mr Blewitt to switch on the music.

The sound system had been specially made by the people who did the rig for *Death Blaster* concerts and tape 36 was awesome: it remixed your dinner inside you; it made old people's hearing-aids overload and their false teeth drop out; it turned even the most iron-lunged baby to gurgling inadequacy; even the young people sometimes had trouble with their belly button studs spinning round and making them look as if they'd got a whirlibug up their T-shirts.

The music blasted the crowd with a roll of sound that blew back their ears and took away all the power from their limbs. It cowed them and it engulfed them.

The only person who moved was the High Priest. Trembling and shivering he tottered forward until he stood in the line with all the vergers and he planted his flabby feet between the golden feet of Ora Himself.

Sebastian watched them all until their hair was standing up on end and then he signalled for the dry ice and the gongs.

It was terrific. Sebastian had always wanted to do something like this, but he'd always held back because of the little children. But there were no little children here: so now he could do anything. He went over to the fireproof cupboard and got out a few handfuls of rockets, just to beef things up.

The dry ice was up to waist height now and tape 36 was reaching its thunderous climax. Sebastian signalled to the dancers. It was really a good thing that the dry ice hid most of Robert and Edward, but Eunice and Mrs Blewitt were fantastic: Eunice was intoning 'Ora, Ora, Ora,' in a deep husky voice while apparently trying to eat her microphone.

The music stabbed once, twice and twice more: *da! da! da-da!* and Sebastian made his run-up to the little trampette, jumped mightily and landed by the Place of Offering just as the last chord sounded. He always enjoyed the shock on everyone's faces when he did that: instantaneous jack-in-the-box effect.

'Hi,' he said, smiling around at the huge shifting mass of people that milled and expanded and were still pushing their way through the huge double doors. 'Welcome to the Temple of Ora, bless His holy name, God of the universe and everything in it.'

A murmur passed over the crowd, but after the music they wouldn't be able to hear what they were saying to each other. It was a good thing he was miked up.

'I'm glad to see you all,' he said, 'because I want to tell

you the Good News.'

They were listening.

'You're all here because there have been some very bad laws passed recently,' he said. 'Stupid, dangerous laws, like the police having Fridays off. Isn't that right?'

A murmur passed over the crowd: half doubt, half hope.

'And I expect you're all wondering what's gone wrong, when Ora and the Sacred Texts have looked after us all so well for so long. Well, I'll tell you.'

There were still people pushing their way in through the rectangle of bright sunshine that marked the doorway, but as soon as they passed through, the great waiting stillness of the crowd flowed over them and they stood quietly, too.

Sebastian waited until people had stopped coming in. There were thousands of eyes staring at him; thousands of flat expectant faces in the soft gold glow of the Temple.

And Sebastian discovered that he had never enjoyed himself so much in his whole life.

'It was the sacred divining rods,' said Sebastian, at last, triumphantly. 'I didn't realize at first–no one did–but they were rigged. Mr Meeno put batteries in them so that the ends lit up at the wrong time. That was why the

Council's laws kept being thrown out and stupid laws kept being passed in their place. And do you know how I found out?'

Sebastian reached into his pocket and brought out a small brown creature that squirmed and quested with a pink and whiffly nose. Sebastian held him up so that everyone could see him and Mr Blewitt, at the control board, put a spotlight on Gerald so that his fur was suddenly transfigured to the purest gold. Gerald, confused, froze: and the crowd gasped.

'This is the Instrument of Ora,' said Sebastian, impressively. 'The sacred rat. It was Gerald that showed me there was something wrong with the divining rods and showed us all the way to get back into Ora's care. And now everything's going to be all right because Mr Meeno's left the City and so we're going to be safe again.'

He paused, then, because he'd lost the crowd. Their eyes had shifted the instant he'd finished speaking and now there were ten thousand eyes gawping at something behind him. He couldn't understand it for a moment, until a golden radiance like a sunrise rose and cast a glow of enveloping warmth that gilded the face of every person in the Temple.

The statue of the god of the City had grown. It was now over a hundred feet high and shining like a star come down from heaven. A gasp of joy and wonder ran through the crowd and many went down on their knees.

Sebastian turned and gave the god of the Golden Temple a thumbs-up.

'Nice one,' he said and Ora smiled and filled the Temple with a thousand rainbows and disappeared.

The crowd went home very quietly, stepping softly, as if they were carrying inside themselves something of the most incredible rarity and preciousness. The High Priest waddled off into a corner so he could sit down and mop his brow; Councillor Kimber and the rest of the Council spent rather a lot of time shaking hands and laughing with grim relief and Sebastian's family retreated to the apprentice's quarters in search of everyday clothes and make-up remover. Mrs Poash, for once, was not one of the last to leave. She marched determinedly up to Horace Meeno, seized him by the elbow and steered him firmly away through the golden doors and out into the sunlight.

In the end only one figure was left before the statue of Ora. It was of a man at the beginning of old age, rather stooped, with jowls that hung in heavy folds around the mouth and sparse combed-over hair that failed to stop his scalp shining faintly gold in the reflected glow of the dome.

He stood and breathed, slowly and heavily, swaying rather, as a man might do at sea.

Finley Wortle.

At long last he whispered 'Whoops!' rather sadly, put a coin in the Bowl of Offering and went home.

Chapter 48

Sebastian Blewitt, apprentice to the High Priest of Ora, paused in the act of slurping his early morning tea. There was a strange thumping out in the corridor, accompanied by heavy and strangled groans.

'High Priest's back from his run,' he observed.

'Bless him,' said Turville, fondly. 'He's got a whole new lease of life since he stood up to that crowd. Got his self-respect back: and he quite *leapt* at the idea of a personal trainer to get him into a bit of a routine. Would you like a biscuit to dunk, dear?'

Sebastian hesitated.

'It's all right,' he said, at last.

'No? Are you sure? What can I get you, then?'

'This is all I need, thanks. It's lovely.'

Turville shook his head disapprovingly.

'You've got to keep your strength up,' he said. 'You've got Mr Walty coming for lessons, later and then you're dirt-track racing and Councillor Kimber is sure to be along with a pile of laws halfway up to the ceiling at some point. Which reminds me: I must make sure everything's all ready for the sacred divining rod checking ceremony later on. Lovely idea, that is: the children will love to see Gerald doing his stuff.

I do like to see the wonder on their little faces.'

'I'll have a really big breakfast,' promised Sebastian and Turville's face lit up.

'What will you have? I've got some lovely blackberries, if you fancy Forest Pancakes –'

'No, no,' said Sebastian, hastily. 'There's no need for you to go to all that trouble. I'll have toast. Lots of toast. That's all I need, honestly.'

Turville put his hands on his hips and as he did one of his gold bracelets flashed.

'Don't you *like* my Forest Pancakes?' he demanded.

Sebastian sat up in bed.

'Yes,' he said, earnestly, 'I do. Really I do. They're perfect.'

Outside a firm voice was saying:

'Right. Now give me twenty and then we'll see if we can find you some turnip juice.' Then more groaning.

'I mean, I want to keep healthy, don't I?' said Sebastian. 'I don't want to end up like Gerald did, or the High Priest. And seeing Councillor Kimber, well, that doesn't take up much energy, does it, especially as I know nothing's going to happen with the divining rods.'

'Shh!' said Turville, coming over all fluttery. 'You're not supposed to say things like that: that's just about the biggest secret in the City.'

'Yeah,' said Sebastian, 'but I can tell you, can't I? You

know everything anyway.'

Turville tut-tutted.

'And that *is* the biggest secret in the City,' he said. 'Oh dear. I knew I shouldn't have let you find out. I knew that my being immortal God would come between us, I just knew it. Oh, it's always the same!'

'But it hasn't made any difference,' said Sebastian. 'I still really like you and everything.'

'Oh yes it has,' said Turville.

'No it hasn't.'

'Oh yes it has.'

Sebastian thought about turkeys and closed his mouth abruptly.

'You see?' said Turville. 'We can't even have a decent argument any more.'

Sebastian sat and felt uncomfortable.

'Perhaps ... perhaps you should get someone else to be High Priest's apprentice,' he suggested, glumly, at last.

'Someone else?' echoed Turville, quite shocked. 'Why? Don't you like it?'

Sebastian thought about not being apprentice; about going back to school. He wouldn't go back to Mr Walty's class, because Mr Walty had been appointed City Crier, a part-time position to go with his duties as Tutor; no, Sebastian would go back to just an ordinary class. He thought about not being in charge of the Temple. Not having people notice him. Not being able to go goldfish racing, or ride on police horses, or slide down the longest banisters in the world at the Grand Theatre.

And he realized that he *loved* being High Priest's apprentice. He wanted more than anything else to stay in the Temple and design a new show that incorporated lots of dangling prisms that would fill the Temple with rainbows just as Ora had done. And he'd had an idea for a smelly display and an official rat patrol.

'That's right,' said Turville, nodding. 'You're a natural, you are: a showman who likes looking after people. You'll be a brilliant High Priest, you will: or a brilliant whatever-you-like.'

Sebastian thought some more. He'd always hoped to be a gangster, but he'd gone off gangsters, just lately. He thought about the Temple itself, dim and echoing and full of a million secret carvings and many millions of careful footfalls, present, and past and yet to come. And of the great golden statue that was the centre of the world and about which all the life in it revolved.

'It's just –' he began; and Turville nodded, understandingly.

'It's just that the thought of living with the immortal, ineffable–that means too good for words, dear– god of the universe really gives you the willies,' he said. 'I do understand. I wasn't at all sure about humans, to begin with: I thought it might all have been a terrible mistake. But, as it turned out, it was actually a tremendously lovely one.'

Sebastian hung his head. He couldn't help thinking it'd be quite peaceful, in a way, to go back to live at home. With Robert and Edward. And Eunice. And Mr and Mrs Blewitt.

'Mm,' said Turville. 'I do see the problem, darling.'

'I'll get used to it,' said Sebastian, glumly. 'To who you are. It's the mind-reading that's a bit difficult, mostly. And ... I suppose you can tell the future, as well, can't you?'

'Well, yes,' said Turville. 'Though on the whole I try not to peek.'

'But there are good things, of course,' went on Sebastian. 'I mean, I bet you even know what frogspawn tastes like.'

Turville laughed.

'Like mouldy ditchwater,' he said.

'Cor, really? Brilliant! I always wanted to know that. See, it's fantastic you being God and all that. Except ... except for knowing you can banish me to an oasis or turn me into a turkey whenever you feel like it. At least, I know you wouldn't, really, of course; well, not unless I really asked for it, anyway.'

Turville smiled a slow smile that was golden, but somehow milky-white at the same time. He raised a slender, beautiful hand and blew carefully at Sebastian along the palm.

'I think you should forget all about it, my love,' he said, very softly and gently.

Sebastian blinked and shook himself, as if from a dream.

Turville was standing waiting: but what for? They'd been having a chat about something, but for the life of him Sebastian couldn't remember what it was all about.

Something important. The dirt-track racing? Or finding the right rats for the new show?

No, it wasn't that. Something else. Something really important.

Ah yes.

'Did you say something about Forest Pancakes?' asked Sebastian, hopefully.

Turville smiled.

'My joy and pleasure, Your Knowingness,' he said.

About the author

I had a fantastic time writing Goldkeeper. Not only did I have all the fun of swaggering around like a gangster, but I got to sniff at things like Mrs Poash. I was even able to send teachers on survival courses, and that's something I'd wanted to do for ages.

I got my own pet rat, too. It was brilliant.

I'm married and have two grown-up daughters. I like to spend my not-writing time walking up hills, or playing the piano, or reading; but it's never long before I'm heading back to my computer to go ... well, absolutely anywhere I like.